Walking Virginia Beach

Katherine Jackson

 Endorsed by the American Volkssport Association

FALCON® HELENA, MONTANA

A FALCON GUIDE®

Falcon® Publishing is continually expanding its list of recreational guide-books. All books include detailed descriptions, accurate maps, and all the information necessary for enjoyable trips. You can order extra copies of this book and get information and prices for other Falcon® guidebooks by writing Falcon, P.O. Box 1718, Helena, MT 59624 or calling toll-free 1-800-582-2665. Also, please ask for a free copy of our current catalog. Visit our website at www.FalconOutdoors.com

Cover photo by Catherine Karnow.

Series editors: Judith Galas and Cindy West.

Library of Congress Cataloging-in-Publication Data

Jackson, Katherine, 1959–
    Walking Virginia Beach / by Katherine Jackson.
        p. cm.
    Includes index.
    ISBN 1-56044-703-6 (pbk.)
    1. Virginia Beach (Va.)—Guidebooks. 2. Walking—Virginia—
Virginia Beach—Guidebooks. I. Title.
F234.V8J33 1999
917.55'510443—dc21   98-51866
                                                                                       CIP

CAUTION

Outdoor recreational activities are by their very nature potentially hazardous. All participants in such activities must assume the responsibility for their own actions and safety. The information contained in this guidebook cannot replace sound judgment and good decision-making skills, which help reduce risk exposure, nor does the scope of this book allow for disclosure of all the potential hazards and risks involved in such activities.

Learn as much as possible about the outdoor recreational activities in which you participate, prepare for the unexpected, and be cautious. The reward will be a safer and more enjoyable experience.

Contents

the walks

The Oceanfront

First Landing/Seashore State Park

Old Princess Anne County

Acknowledgments

This book was enriched by my friends and colleagues in Virginia Beach, who love their city. At the City of Virginia Beach, the Public Information Office provided a wealth of information, and city photographer, Carole Arnold, opened her photography files to me. My buddies at the Public Library Department, Visitor Center, Convention and Visitor Development, Economic Development, and Barker Campbell Farley & Mansfield shared photos, brochures, and press kits. Phillip Roehrs of Public Works provided immeasurable encouragement and acted as liaison with the Mapping Division, which provided many maps. Deb Perry provided information and photos from the Virginia Marine Science Museum, and staff from Parks and Recreation provided information and maps for the parks. The Department of Planning provided a map and information on the Elizabeth River walk. The volunteers and staff of First Landing/Seashore State Park and Back Bay National Wildlife Refuge deserve recognition for the information they provided on Virginia Beach's natural areas.

I also appreciate the fine service I received in Norfolk from the Division of Surveys and the Convention and Visitors Bureau. Hampton Conventions and Tourism assisted with the Hampton walk. Colonial Williamsburg Foundation, the National Park Service, and the Association for the Preservation of Virginia Antiquities provided information, maps, and photos.

I referred to numerous reference books on the history and natural resources of the area. Among them were Stephen Mansfield's *Princess Anne County and Virginia Beach: A Pictorial History; The Beach: A History of Virginia Beach, Virginia*, revised by the Virginia Beach Public Library; Alice

Jane Lippson and Robert L. Lippson's book *Life in the Chesapeake Bay;* and *Norfolk, Virginia: The Sunrise City by the Sea* by Amy Waters Yarinske.

I also appreciate my Virginia Beach neighbors, who shared their stories.

For all my buddies, Who encouraged me, walked
with me, or put up with me on deadline.
And for my mom, Barbara Weatherford Martin.

*"The cure for anything is salt water—sweat, tears,
or the sea."*

–Isak Dinesen

Foreword

For almost 20 years, Falcon has guided millions of people to America's wild outside, showing them where to paddle, hike, bike, bird, fish, climb, and drive. With this walking series, we at Falcon ask you to try something just as adventurous. We invite you to experience this country from its sidewalks, not its back roads, and to stroll through some of America's most interesting cities.

In their haste to get where they are going, travelers often bypass this country's cities, and in the process, they miss the historic and scenic treasures hidden among the bricks. Many people seek spectacular scenery and beautiful settings on top of the mountains, along the rivers, and in the woods. While nothing can replace the serenity and inspiration of America's natural wonders, we should not overlook the beauty of the urban landscape.

The steel and glass of municipal mountains reflect the sunlight and make people feel small in the shadows. Birds sing in city parks, water burbles in the fountains, and along the sidewalks walkers can still see abundant wildlife—their fellow human beings.

Falcon's many outdoor guidebooks have encouraged people not only to explore and enjoy America's natural beauty but to preserve and protect it. Our cities also are meant to be enjoyed and explored, and their irreplaceable treasures need care and protection.

When travelers and walkers want to explore something that is inspirational and beautiful, we hope they will lace up their walking shoes and point their feet toward one of this country's many cities.

For there, along the walkways, they are sure to discover the excitement, history, beauty, and charm of urban America.

—*The Editors*

Map Legend

Walk Route, paved		Food Service	
Walk Route, unpaved		Observation Deck	
Walk Route, boardwalk		Tennis Courts	
Interstate Highway		Overlook	
Street or Road		River or Stream	
Hiking/Walking Trail		Waterfall	
Start/Finish of Loop Walk	S/F	Lake or Pond	
Parking Area	P	Park or Garden Area	
Building		Interstate Highway	64
Church or Cathedral		U.S. Highway	60
Restrooms, Male and Female		State or County Road	44
Wheelchair Access		Map Orientation	N
Picnic Area		Scale of Distance	0 0.5 1 Miles
Playground			

Overview Map

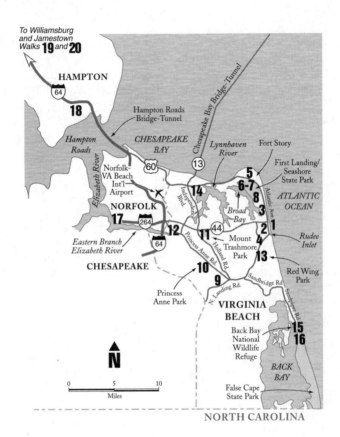

Preface: Come Walk Virginia Beach

With 38 miles of coastline, an oceanfront boardwalk, three wildlife refuges, and more than 200 parks, Virginia Beach offers miles of walking paths to explore. You can begin in the resort area, where the historic "Boardwalk," now a wide, concrete promenade, extends 2.5 miles along the Atlantic Ocean. Here you will see the beauty Virginia Beach is known for, with dramatic sunrises over the ocean and brilliant sunsets over Rudee Inlet. You will stroll by quaint beach cottages from the turn of the 20th century and elegant oceanfront mansions.

Then walk through the parks and neighborhoods to get an understanding of the current and historic value of the rivers and bays that connect Virginia Beach with Chesapeake Bay and the Atlantic Ocean. These bodies of water provided important transportation links in colonial days. Today, they form a playground for water-sports enthusiasts. Breathtaking landscapes and wild creatures can be seen along these shores. You will wander through cypress swamps and hardwood forests, new neighborhoods and old.

Walks in neighboring cities will provide lessons on colonial Virginia. After seeing the place where the *Susan Constant*, *Godspeed*, and *Discovery* landed at the mouth of the Chesapeake Bay in Virginia Beach, you can follow their route up the James River, passing Norfolk and Hampton. You can explore Jamestown Island, site of the first permanent English settlement, and Williamsburg, the colonial capital.

The best way to get to know a city is on foot. If you are visiting Virginia Beach for the first time, *Walking Virginia Beach* will introduce you to the history and scenic splendor of this oceanfront city. If you live in the city or are visiting again, *Walking Virginia Beach* will help you explore new areas. Use all your senses as you walk to discover the sights, smells, and sounds of Virginia Beach.

Stretching for 2.5 miles along the oceanfront, from Rudee Inlet to 40th Street, the Virginia Beach Boardwalk is the place to see and be seen. PHOTO COURTESY OF VIRGINIA BEACH CONVENTION AND VISITOR DEVELOPMENT

Introduction

Walking the streets and boulevards of a city can take you into its heart and give you a feel for its pulse and personality. From the sidewalk looking up, you can appreciate its architecture. From the sidewalk peeking in, you can find the quaint shops, local museums, and great eateries that give a city its charm and personality. From its nature paths, you can smell the flowers, glimpse the wildlife, gaze at a lake, or hear a creek gurgle. Only by walking can you get close enough to read the historical plaques and watch the people. When you walk a city, you get it all—adventure, scenery, local color, good exercise, and fun.

How to use this guide

We have designed this book so that you can easily find the walks that match your interests, time, and energy level. The Trip Planner is the first place you should look when deciding on a walk. This table will give you the basic information—a walk's distance, the estimated walking time, and the difficulty. The pictures or icons in the table also tell you specific things about the walk:

Every walk has something of interest, but this icon tells you that the route will have particular appeal to the shutterbug. Bring your camera. You will have great views of the city or the surrounding area, and you are likely to get some great scenic shots.

Somewhere along the route you will have the chance to get food or a beverage. You will have to glance through the walk description to determine where and what kind of food and beverages are available. Walks that do not have the food icon probably are along nature trails or in noncommercial areas of the city.

During your walk you will have the chance to shop. More detailed descriptions of the types of stores you will find can be found in the actual walk description.

This walk features something kids will enjoy seeing or doing—a park, zoo, museum, or play equipment. In most cases the walks that carry this icon are short and follow an easy, fairly level path. You know your young walking companions best. If your children are patient walkers who do not tire easily, then feel free to choose walks that are longer and harder. In fact, depending on a child's age and energy, most children can do any of the walks in this book. The icon only notes those walks we think they will especially enjoy.

Your path will take you primarily through urban areas. Buildings, small city parks, and paved paths are what you will see and pass.

You will pass through a large park or walk in a natural setting where you can see and enjoy nature.

The wheelchair icon means that the path is fully accessible. This walk would be easy for someone pushing a wheelchair or stroller. We have made every attempt to follow a high standard for accessibility. The icon means there are curb cuts or ramps along the entire route, plus a wheelchair-accessible bathroom somewhere along the way. The path is mostly or entirely paved, and ramps and unpaved surfaces are clearly described. If you use a wheelchair and have the ability to negotiate curbs and dirt paths or to wheel for longer distances and on uneven surfaces, you may want to skim the directions for the walks that do not carry this symbol. You may find other walks you will enjoy. If in doubt, read the full text of the walk or call the contact source for guidance.

Joggers also are likely to enjoy many of the walks in this book. All walks are easy and most have level routes and paved or smooth surfaces.

At the start of each walk chapter, you will find specific information describing the route and what you can expect on your walk:

General location: Here you will get the walk's general location in the city or within a specific area.

Special attractions: Look here to find the specific things you will pass. If this walk has museums, historic homes, restaurants, or wildlife, it will be noted here.

Difficulty: For this book, we have selected walking routes that an average person in reasonable health can complete easily. In most cases, you will be walking on flat surfaces with few, if any, hills. Your path will most likely be a maintained surface of concrete, asphalt, wood, or packed dirt. It will be easy to follow, and you will be only a block or so from a phone, other people, or businesses. If the walk is less than a mile, you may be able to walk comfortably in street shoes. If you are in doubt about whether you can manage a particular walk, read the description carefully or call the listed contact for more information.

Distance and estimated time: This gives the total distance of the walk. The time allotted for each walk is based on walking time only, which we have calculated at about 30 minutes per mile, a slow pace. Most people have no trouble walking a mile in half an hour, and people with some walking experience often walk a 20-minute mile. If the walk includes museums, shops, or restaurants, you may want to add sightseeing time to the estimate.

Services: Here you will find out if such things as restrooms, parking, refreshments, or information centers are available and where you are likely to find them.

Public transportation: Many cities have excellent transportation systems; others have limited services. If it is possible to take a bus or commuter train to the walk's starting point, you will find the bus or train noted here. You may also find some information about where the bus or train stops and how often and when it runs.

The walk

When you reach this point, you are ready to start walking. In this section you will find not only specific and detailed directions, but you will also learn more about the things you are passing. Those who want only the directions and none of the extras can find the straightforward directions by looking for the ➤.

What to wear

The best advice is to wear something comfortable. Leave behind anything that binds, pinches, rides up, falls down, slips off the shoulder, or comes undone. Otherwise, let common sense, the weather, and your own body tell you what to wear.

What to take

Be sure to take water. Strap a bottle to your fanny pack or tuck a small one in a pocket. If you are walking several miles with a dog, remember to take a small bowl so your pet can have a drink, too.

Carry some water even if you will be walking where refreshments are available. Several small sips taken throughout a walk are more effective than one large drink at the walk's end. Avoid drinks with caffeine or alcohol because they deplete rather than replenish your body's fluids.

Safety and street savvy

Mention a big city and many people immediately think of safety. Is it safe to walk there during the day? What about at night? Are there areas I should avoid?

You should use common sense whether you are walking in a small town or a big city, but safety does not have to be your overriding concern. American cities are enjoyable places, and you will find that they are also safe places.

Any safety mishap in a large city is likely to involve petty theft or vandalism. So, the biggest tip is simple: Do not tempt thieves. Purses dangling on shoulder straps or slung over your arm, wallets peeking out of pockets, arms burdened with packages, valuables on the car seat—all of these things attract the pickpocket, purse snatcher, or thief. If you look like you could easily be relieved of your possessions, you may be.

Do not carry a purse. Put your money in a money belt or tuck your wallet into a deep side pocket of your pants or skirt or in a fanny pack that rides over your hip or stomach. Lock your valuables in the trunk of your car before you park and leave for your walk. Protect your camera by wearing the strap across your chest, not just over your shoulder. Better yet, put your camera in a backpack.

You also will feel safer if you remember the following:
- Be aware of your surroundings and the people near you.
- Avoid parks or other isolated places at night.
- Walk with others.
- Walk in well-lit and well-traveled areas.

The walks in this book were selected by people who had safety in mind. No walk will take you through a bad neighborhood or into an area of the city that is known to be dangerous. So relax and enjoy your walk.

Trip Planner

the walks

Walk name	Difficulty	Distance (miles)	Time	♿	🏢	🌿	🌸	👤	📖	🛒	📷
The Oceanfront											
1. The Resort Town	easy	4	2 hrs	✓		✓	✓	✓		✓	✓
2. Rudee Inlet	easy	2	1 hr			✓	✓		✓	✓	✓
3. The North End	moderate	6	3 hrs			✓	✓		✓	✓	✓
4. Owls Creek Salt Marsh	easy	1	45 mins	✓		✓	✓	✓	✓	✓	✓
First Landing/Seashore State Park											
5. First Landing and First Lighthouse	easy	1	45 mins			✓	✓	✓	✓		✓
6. Bald Cypress Trail	moderate	1.5	1 hr			✓	✓	✓			
7. Broad Bay	difficult	6	4.5 hrs			✓	✓				✓
8. The Narrows	moderate	3.5	2 hrs			✓	✓	✓	✓		✓
Old Princess Anne County											
9. The Courthouse	easy	1.25	45 mins	✓	✓		✓	✓		✓	
10. Farmer's Market	easy	2	1 hr	✓	✓		✓		✓	✓	
In the Parks											
11. Mount Trashmore Park	easy	2	1 hr		✓		✓	✓			✓

6

	Difficulty	Distance	Time	Wheelchair access	City setting	Nature setting	Good for kids	Shopping	Food	Bring camera
12. The Elizabeth River	easy	2	1 hr							✓
13. Red Wing Park Gardens	moderate	2.5	1.5 hrs			✓			✓	✓
In the Neighborhoods										
14. Historic Houses on the River	easy	2	1 hr					✓		
Back Bay National Wildlife Refuge										
15. Back Bay	easy	1	30 mins			✓	✓		✓	✓
16. Beaches and Dikes	difficult	6.5	3.5 hrs			✓			✓	✓
Neighboring Cities										
17. Norfolk	moderate	4	2 hrs					✓	✓	✓
18. Hampton	easy	2.5	1.5 hrs				✓	✓	✓	✓
19. Colonial Williamsburg	easy	2.5	1.5 hrs					✓	✓	✓
20. Jamestown	easy	1.25	1.5 hrs						✓	✓

the icons

Wheelchair access   City setting   Nature setting   Good for kids   Shopping   Food   Bring camera

Meet Virginia Beach

General

    Time Zone: Eastern Standard Time

    Area Code: 757

Size

    Virginia's most populous city

    Approximately 430,000 people

    259 square miles of land

    51 square miles of water

Elevation

    Average 12 feet above sea level

Climate

    Average yearly precipitation: 36 inches, mostly rain

    Average temperatures in April: high 67 degrees F, low 41 degrees F

    Average temperatures in July: high 87 degrees F, low 72 degrees F

    Average temperatures in September: high 80 degrees F, low 67 degrees F

    Average water temperature in July: 78 degrees F

Major highways

    Interstate: 64

    U.S. highways: 13, 17, 58

Airport service

    Flights to Norfolk International Airport on USAirways, Delta, Continental, American, Northwest, United

Recreation

    Golf courses: 12 public

    Parks: 2 state parks, 1 national wildlife refuge, 198 city parks

Scenic waterway: 79 miles
Coastline: 38 miles
Bikeways: 60 miles
Tennis courts: 194
Marinas: 54 with public access

Major industries

Conventions and tourism, telecommunications, agribusiness, military, retail and wholesale distribution.

Media

Television stations

ABC—Channel 13
NBC—Channel 10
CBS—Channel 3
FOX—Channel 43
PBS—Channel 15

Radio stations

WCMS 100.5 FM—country
WFOG 92.9 FM—easy listening
WHRO 90.3 FM—classical
WHRV 89.5 FM—National Public Radio, alternative
WJCD 105.3 FM—jazz
WKOC 93.7 FM—modern hits
WLTY 95.7 FM—oldies
WNIS 850 AM—all news/weather/talk
WOWI 103 FM—urban
WPTE 94.9 FM—alternative and modern rock
WTAR 790 AM—talk

Newspapers

The Virginian-Pilot, morning daily
Virginia Beach Sun, weekly

Special annual events

Call 757-491-SUNN or 800-446-8038 for recorded information, or access Virginia Beach websites: www.virginia-beach.va.us and www.vbfun.com.

- January–February: Whale-watching boat tours
- February: Mid-Atlantic Wildfowl Festival, Pavilion Convention Center
- March: Shamrock Marathon and Sportsfest, including a fitness walk, on the oceanfront
- Easter: Sunrise service, Fort Story; Eggstravaganza at 24th Street Park
- April: Historic Garden Week, various locations in Virginia Beach; The Virginia Waterfront International Arts Festival, various locations throughout the area
- May: Beach Music Festival, Big Band Weekend, and Viva Elvis Festival, on the oceanfront; Strawberry Festival, Pungo.
- June: Boardwalk Art Show; Harborfest, Norfolk; Jazz Festival, Hampton
- July 4: Family Fun Day with Fireworks, Mount Trashmore Park
- August: East Coast Surfing Championships, on the oceanfront
- Labor Day: American Music Festival, on the oceanfront
- September: Neptune Festival, on the oceanfront
- October: African-American Festival of Pride, 24th Street Park; Blues at the Beach, 17th Street Park
- November–December: Holiday Lights at the Beach, on the Boardwalk

Weather

Virginia Beach enjoys pleasant weather year-round. January and February temperatures generally hover in the 40s, but occasional 60- or 70-degree days are a special treat. With proper outerwear, walking in all types of weather only adds to the experience of the ocean, the woods, and the parks. A midweight winter coat should suffice for warmth, especially since you will generate heat while walking. The woods of the First Landing/Seashore State Park and the Elizabeth River walks provide sheltered paths on windy days. The best part of winter walking is that you often have the walkways all to yourself.

During the middle of summer, temperatures can soar into the 90s and humidity can be high. However, pleasant 75-degree F days also occur. Lightweight, loose clothing is recommended. Drinking plenty of water is important on any walk but particularly during the heat and humidity of the summer. You may want to plan your walk to take advantage of cool mornings and evenings or take shady wooded walks during the heat of the day.

Spring and fall are glorious in Virginia Beach, with ideal temperatures in the 60s or 70s. Layering clothes will allow you to adjust to any temperature. A light jacket or sweatshirt will probably provide all the warmth you will need.

The Atlantic hurricane season lasts from June 1 to November 30, and most tropical-storm activity occurs in the fall. Hurricanes, which often skirt the coast, and northeaster storms, which hit in the winter, can bring high winds and torrential downpours. The Weather Channel provides adequate warning and hourly updates during hurricane season. Keeping an eye on the weather during this season is important.

Transportation

By car: Virginia Beach is a large city, but a significant portion of it remains rural. The city is easy to get around by car. The Virginia Beach/Norfolk Expressway (Route 44) is the main artery from which most walks can be accessed. Route 44 becomes 21st Street as it enters the oceanfront resort area (and 22nd Street as it leaves the oceanfront).

Atlantic Avenue is the main thoroughfare at the oceanfront. It can be congested at the south end during the summer, but Pacific Avenue, which runs parallel to it, is also available for north-south travel. Shore Drive (Virginia Route 60) runs along the shore of Chesapeake Bay and provides beautiful views as well as access to several walks.

Interstate 64 provides access to Virginia Beach and to walks in the neighboring cities of Norfolk, Hampton, Williamsburg, and Jamestown. You can reach Virginia Beach from the north via Virginia Route 13, which includes the scenic Chesapeake Bay Bridge-Tunnel. Route 13 saves 95 miles and costs $10 one-way. From the south, U.S. Highways 58 and 17 connect to I-64.

Parking at the oceanfront is available in municipal and private parking lots and at on-street meters. The meters are stringently monitored during the summer but are free during the winter.

By bus: Greyhound and Trailways Bus Lines provide service into the area. Tidewater Regional Transit (TRT) provides local public transportation. Many TRT buses are wheelchair accessible.

By air: Norfolk–Virginia Beach International Airport offers 200 daily flights. The airport is located off I-64 and is served by most major carriers. Most national car rental companies also offer service at the airport. The airport is about 20 miles, or a $25 cab fare, from the beach.

By train: Amtrak service is available to Newport News, Virginia. Passengers can travel by bus from there to the heart of the Virginia Beach resort area.

Safety

Virginia Beach is one of the safest cities of its size in the country, according to FBI statistics. A well-trained police force and a focus on community-policing programs contribute to the city's safety. You should not have to worry about your safety in Virginia Beach if you follow basic safety precautions. Park in recommended areas and lock your car doors when you leave.

The best time to take the walks in this book is during daylight hours. Most parks close at sunset, so you cannot walk in them after dark. You can walk along the Boardwalk in the oceanfront area in the evening, because the Boardwalk is well lit. The Hampton, Norfolk, and Williamsburg walks are also lit, so you can take them in the evening but you will miss some of their scenic beauty in the dark.

While walking, be aware of the possibility of dehydration, sunburn, and heat exhaustion. To protect yourself from the sun whenever you are outdoors, use a sunscreen with a rating of SPF 15 or higher. Make sure that it protects against UVA and UVB rays. You may also want to consider wearing a hat, long sleeves, and pants, but keep in mind that the sun can penetrate clothing.

To prevent dehydration, drink plenty of liquids that do not contain alcohol or caffeine. Water is available along some of the walking routes in this book. Carrying your own supply is always a good idea. Most sources recommend that you drink 64 ounces of water each day. On days when you exercise, you will want to drink more.

During the summer, consider walking during the cooler mornings and early evenings, especially on the walks along the oceanfront, at Back Bay, and in neighboring cities. The walking routes in First Landing/Seashore State Park are predominantly wooded and are a good choice on sunny summer days.

In the summer, ticks haunt the woods of Virginia Beach. After a walk in the woods, you should carefully check your hair and body for ticks. If you find one, remove it with tweezers, being careful to remove the entire insect. Your dog can also pick up ticks. During the summer, mosquitoes are also plentiful in the woods, especially in areas near the water. Consider carrying insect repellent.

Finally, always be aware of traffic and yield the right-of-way in every case. Choose clothing that announces your presence to motorists, but be aware that they will not always see you. Obey all traffic signals, and walk on the opposite side of the road facing traffic if there is no sidewalk.

Accommodations

Virginia Beach offers every sort of accommodation imaginable, from 11,000 rooms in large and small hotels to guest houses, rental cottages, and campgrounds. The Virginia Beach Visitor Information Center offers a central reservations system for oceanfront hotels. First Landing/Seashore State Park has tent sites in its campground, as well as small cabins. Rental cottages are available through various real-estate companies in the city. The Virginia Beach Visitor Information Center, 800-VA-BEACH, can direct you to the accommodations that best suit your needs.

The Story of Virginia Beach

When 104 Englishmen crossed the Atlantic Ocean on the *Susan Constant*, *Godspeed*, and *Discovery* and landed in the New World in 1607, they found a place of wild beauty, lush forests, and sheltered bays. Scouting parties explored the cypress forests, the sandy dunes, and the winding waterways. They encountered Chesapeake Indians, who hunted and fished the bounteous land. The Englishmen ate their first oysters and picked strawberries four times larger than those in their native country. They claimed the new land for the British crown and named their landing site Cape Henry in honor of King James's son Henry, Prince of Wales.

Several days after landing, the colonists sailed up Chesapeake Bay until they found what they believed to be a safe area for settlement. This site on the James River became Jamestown, the first permanent English settlement in the New World.

During the 1600s and 1700s, the population near this "First Landing" site, which would later become Princess Anne County and Virginia Beach, gradually increased as more English settlers came to the Virginia Colony hoping to find prosperity. Many colonists, such as Adam Thoroughgood, were awarded 100 acres of land for every person whose passage they paid from England. Plantations were established, often on the shores of the rivers and bays, that became the colonial highways. As the plantations flourished, they were grouped into counties for governance. Princess Anne County was established in 1691 and named for the younger daughter of James II and Anne Hyde.

In the late 1800s, the U.S. Life-Saving Service constructed a network of life-saving stations to serve ships sailing along the Atlantic Coast. The Seatack Life-Saving Station was built in what is now the heart of Virginia Beach. A small settlement grew up around the station, as life-saving servicemen built homes nearby for their families. These early residents saved the lives of thousands of sailors whose ships became stranded offshore.

Meanwhile, the neighboring city of Norfolk had grown and prospered, due in part to its location on one of the largest natural harbors in the world. In 1883, a group of businessmen, realizing the recreational appeal of the Atlantic Ocean and its sandy shore, built a rail system to bring visitors from Norfolk to the coast, where Colonel Marshall Parks had built the beach's first wooden clubhouse. A year later, the first hotel in Virginia Beach opened. Families built cottages north and south of the hotel and spent summers relaxing on the beach. Large guesthouses and other hotels soon opened, inaugurating a tradition of hospitality that has thrived in Virginia Beach ever since. In 1906, the fledgling resort community incorporated and became the town of Virginia Beach.

Throughout the early 1900s, Virginia Beach's reputation as an East Coast resort grew, and nightclubs, such as the Peacock Club, became regular stops on the circuits of such well-known performers as Cab Calloway, Duke Ellington, and Glenn Miller. When the Cavalier Hotel opened in 1927, the governor of Virginia declared it the best resort hotel in America. Distinguished guests, including F. Scott Fitzgerald, Fatty Arbuckle, and Victor Borge, helped to spread the word.

The U.S. military played a significant role in the development of Virginia Beach. Since World War II, army, navy, and national guard commands have operated within the city limits. Today, the Little Creek Amphibious Training Command is the largest base of its kind in the world. Naval Air Station Oceana is one of the most important jet bases in the nation. Military installations provide jobs for residents and incentives for businesses to locate in the city. The city also benefits from a strong tradition of volunteerism and community service among military personnel.

In 1963, the small resort town of Virginia Beach and sprawling Princess Anne County merged to become the City of Virginia Beach. For many years, the city was considered a bedroom community for people who worked at the businesses and military bases in Norfolk. Virginia Beach has since come into its own as the most populous city in the state, with a new sense of identity as an ideal place to work, live, and play. The municipal government has focused on developing educational resources and recreational amenities, such as golf courses and entertainment venues. These are intended to appeal not only to residents and visitors but also to corporations looking for a place to locate.

Fortunately for Virginia Beach residents and visitors, the city is rich in parks and conservation areas, including a national wildlife refuge and two large state parks. At the same time the population exploded in the 1980s, planners focused on the creation and preservation of parks and open spaces. In the mid-1900s, the city purchased a tract of land in the geographic center of Virginia Beach that is larger than Central Park in New York City. It was earmarked for recreational and educational development. A golf course, amphitheater, and sports stadium have been built on this property, and sites have been designated for several schools.

Each year, 2.5 million visitors join residents in enjoying the natural beauty of Virginia Beach and the various festivals and events that are offered at the oceanfront and in the parks. In 1998, *Money* magazine named Virginia Beach and its environs the best big city in the South. The Virginia Marine Science Museum is one of the top-ten most popular marine science and aquarium facilities in the country, and the oceanfront Boardwalk has been heralded in national magazines and *USA Today* as one of the best walks in the country.

The walks in this book will introduce you to the treasures of Virginia Beach. Take time to stop along the way and chat with the people who live here. You will find the spirit of warm, Southern hospitality thriving at "The Beach," a place that has been called the biggest small town you will ever love.

Nearly 400 years ago, 104 Englishmen recognized the region's appeal when they disembarked from their ships and began to explore. Your adventures in Virginia Beach will show you why one of them, Captain George Percy, wrote in his journal that he was "ravished" at the sight of the "fair meadows," "goodly tall trees," and "fresh waters" running through the woods.

of interest

A tradition of service

Some of the earliest residents of Virginia Beach devoted their lives to serving others, and that tradition of service continues today.

The U.S. Life-Saving Service was established in the 1870s under President Ulysses Grant. "Surfmen" at stations up and down the Atlantic Coast patrolled the beach, watching for shipwrecks and bravely saving lives. In Virginia Beach, five stations guarded the beach at 5- to 7-mile intervals. On clear days, surfmen could stand on the beach by their stations and see all the way to the next one. At each station, 40-foot towers were manned 24 hours a day. Throughout the night, and whenever the weather limited visibility during the day, surfmen took turns patrolling the beach between the stations on foot and later on horseback.

The surfmen had several ways to rescue stranded sailors. They used a Lyle gun to fire a line to ships up to 700 yards away. The gun worked like a cannon with a fuse and fire, ejecting a 30-pound weight aimed at the mast of the grounded ship. But unlike a cannonball, this projectile was attached to a rope. When it hit the ship, the crew could fasten the line to the rigging, and a breeches buoy could be ferried out. This buoy was a large life ring with a pair of canvas breeches attached to the underside. A stranded sailor would put his legs through the holes in the breeches and sit in the sling with his arms over the ring. Suspended from a line between the ship's rigging and a pair of poles crossed in the sand on the beach, the sailor could be brought to safety. A lifecar, which would carry more than one sailor at a time, could be ferried to ships on a similar line.

If conditions allowed, the station keeper would order his crew to get out the 27-foot surfboat. While the keeper barked orders, the crew would row the wooden boat through the breakers toward the stranded ship. When they reached it, they would either load the sailors into the surfboat or climb onto the marooned ship to attach a line for the breeches buoy.

In 1915, the U.S. Life-Saving Service was reorganized as the Coast Guard. As ships became safer and navigational equipment improved, the need for the life-saving stations declined. They were sold for conversion into homes or occasionally preserved as museums, like the Old Coast Guard Station at 24th Street.

A tradition of community service remains strong in Virginia Beach. Ten thousand volunteers contribute 1.5 million hours of service annually to the city. Virginia Beach volunteer programs have been viewed as models by municipalities around the country, as well as by foreign governments. The city boasts the largest all-volunteer rescue service in the nation. Hundreds of volunteers staff the Virginia Marine Science Museum. Citizen-police academies contribute to community safety. Library volunteers restock bookshelves, and young people serve as mentors to their peers.

walk 1

The Resort Town

General location: The walk begins on the oceanfront Boardwalk, meanders through the beach borough, and ends on Atlantic Avenue.

Special attractions: Atlantic Wildfowl Heritage Museum, Old Coast Guard Station, fishing pier, Contemporary Art Center of Virginia, Tidewater Veterans Memorial.

Difficulty rating: Easy; flat, paved surfaces; accessible to people with disabilities.

Distance: 4 miles.

Estimated time: 2 hours.

Services: Accessible public restrooms at 17th and 24th Streets, restaurants, visitor information center and kiosk, water fountains along the Boardwalk.

The Resort Town

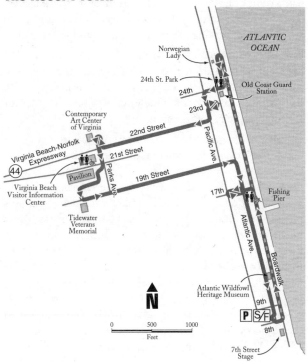

Restrictions: Pets are not allowed on the Boardwalk or the grassy area east of Atlantic Avenue from May through September. Leashed pets are permitted during the off-season; all droppings must be picked up.

For more information: Contact the Virginia Beach Visitor Information Center.

Getting started: The Virginia Beach oceanfront is at the eastern end of Virginia Beach/Norfolk Expressway (Route 44), which becomes 21st Street as you enter the beach borough. Turn right onto Pacific Avenue and drive south 12 blocks. Turn left at the traffic light on 9th Street and then right into the 9th Street parking garage. Fees vary with the seasons.

Public transportation: Trolleys run up and down Atlantic Avenue during the summer season. Bus service is available to the oceanfront via Tidewater Regional Transit Routes 20, 24, 29, and 33. Contact Tidewater Regional Transit for schedule and fare information.

Overview: This walk explores the heart of the Virginia Beach oceanfront resort area, where reminders of the city's maritime history mix with salt air and ocean breezes. During the late 1800s, the seed for what would eventually grow into a vacation destination for 2.5 million visitors a year was planted by a local developer, Colonel Marshall Parks. Parks built a wooden clubhouse on the oceanfront near what is now 17th Street. Shortly thereafter, a railway was built from the nearby city of Norfolk to the oceanfront, and the 75-guest Virginia Beach Hotel opened. Within a few years, the property around the hotel was subdivided and sold for the construction of beach cottages. The original hotel, renamed the Princess Anne Hotel, was extended from what is now 14th to 16th Streets, and it began to attract world-class performers and up to 400 guests at a time. Celebrities and statesmen including Benjamin Harrison, Grover Cleveland, Alexander Graham Bell, and John Barrymore traveled to the small resort to enjoy the healthy sea air and the mild weather.

The town was incorporated in 1906, and even though its main attraction, the exclusive hotel, burned in 1907, the resort continued to grow. More hotels grew up along the coast. Today, the resort strip boasts approximately 8,000 hotel rooms, and several new hotels are on the way. Visitors still come to the area to enjoy the sand and sea, but the tourist industry has expanded to include amenities such as golf courses, an amphitheater, museums, marinas, and other sporting and entertainment facilities. This walk showcases the early resort area and modern attractions.

The walk

➤Leave the parking garage by the stairs in the southeast corner. You will emerge at the corner of Atlantic Avenue and 8th Street. Cross Atlantic and follow the blue brick pavement to the Boardwalk. The fish sculptures you see in this side-street connector park were part of a $60 million renovation of Atlantic that occurred in the 1990s.

As you reach the Boardwalk, you will see on your right the 7th Street Stage, a popular fair-weather gathering place that is included in the Rudee Inlet walk (see walk 2). To continue the Resort Town walk, turn left onto the Board-walk. You will walk north for 17 blocks.

➤Continue walking north along the Boardwalk. At 15th Street, the Virginia Beach Fishing Pier stretches out into the Atlantic Ocean, welcoming anglers who catch spot, croaker, bluefish, and an occasional flounder. For those who do not fish, a stroll along the pier is worthwhile for the view. Directly across the Boardwalk, a small amusement area offers children's rides and games during the summer.

This area was the site of the early Princess Anne Hotel and the birthplace of the resort area. At 17th Street, where the first clubhouse was built on the oceanfront, a public park and stage now provide a setting for nightly live entertain-ment during the summer. A tourist information kiosk and accessible public restrooms are available here.

The Virginia Beach Boardwalk

Built in 1888, the original Virginia Beach Boardwalk was a wooden promenade extending 4 blocks south from the Princess Anne Hotel. A fire that destroyed the grand hotel also consumed most of the Boardwalk. Twenty years later, a $250,000 bond issue funded a new concrete walkway. The walkway was lengthened in 1938 and 1939, and it currently extends from Rudee Inlet to 40th Street, a distance of approximately 2.5 miles. A new project to construct a seawall from Rudee Inlet to 58th Street includes a renovation of the Boardwalk. The section from Rudee Inlet to 8th Street is now complete, and additional portions of the project, which includes storm-water pumping stations, will be built in years to come. In addition to providing erosion control and hurricane protection to the businesses, residences, and streets west of the seawall, the project will provide a new and enhanced promenade for beach goers to enjoy.

The Boardwalk is the most popular place in Virginia Beach for biking, skating, and strolling. There is nightly entertainment during the summer and on weekends during the spring and fall. You might wander into an outdoor theatrical performance, a classical music concert, an acoustic performance, or a troupe of wandering clowns. The Boardwalk is also the site of large festivals, such as the Boardwalk Art Festival, held in June and considered one of the top outdoor art festivals in the country. The Neptune Festival, which takes place the last weekend in September, is the Virginia Beach version of Mardi Gras. The American Music Festival on Labor Day weekend features national entertainers performing on a giant stage built on the beach. Sign boxes along the Boardwalk provide information on current and upcoming events.

of interest

The Atlantic Wildfowl Heritage Museum

The DeWitt Cottage, the first brick house designed for year-round living at the resort, was built at 11th Street and Atlantic Avenue in 1895 by B. P. Holland, the first mayor and postmaster of Virginia Beach. The brick cottage is now listed on the National Register of Historic Places. The DeWitts bought the house in 1909, and members of the family occupied it until 1988.

In 1995, the cottage was renovated to house the Atlantic Wildfowl Heritage Museum, which is run by the Back Bay Wildfowl Guild. The museum exhibits an impressive array of hand-carved and painted decoys of the migratory waterfowl that visit eastern Virginia. Visitors can learn about the history of the craft—from the earliest Native American decoys to contemporary, award-winning works. The museum also houses a small gift shop and offers educational programs and decoy workshops.

►Turn left and take a short detour down the first block of 17th Street to see a cluster of early 20th-century commercial buildings, some of which have had facelifts over the years. The two-story brick structures, such as the building with the parapet on the southeast corner of 17th Street and Pacific Avenue and the mission-style structure with the curved parapet on the north side of the street, are reminiscent of the early commercial architecture in this area. The mission-style building once housed the Roland Theater.

►Return to the Boardwalk and turn left. Stop at some point and use the binoculars mounted along the walkway to get a closer look at the barges, boats, and other watercraft that share the ocean.

The Old Coast Guard Station

Built in 1903, the Old Coast Guard Station was one of a network of lifesaving stations that Congress authorized in the 1870s to render assistance to ships in peril. It is the only station still open in Virginia, and it is now a museum dedicated to the history of the U.S. Life-Saving Service, the forerunner of the Coast Guard. It is on the National Register of Historic Places.

The museum features the history of 600 shipwrecks along the Virginia coast, as well as exhibits of rescue equipment and other elements of maritime history. Visitors can relive the victories and the defeats of daring surfmen who braved the wild and often frigid waters of the Atlantic to rescue crewmen of ships stranded on sandbars or in shallow waters. Outside the museum, anchors and timbers from sunken ships are on display.

Adjacent to the Old Coast Guard Station is 24th Street Park, a monument to what citizens can accomplish by banding together in a common cause. This lot, one of the last remaining stretches of open space along the oceanfront, was to be the site of a new hotel. However, a group of citizens convinced the city council to preserve the area as a public park. The citizens' group raised hundreds of thousands of dollars, which were combined with city funds to build the park and stage. The picturesque wooden architecture reflects the style of the Old Coast Guard Station, and the stage and park are popular places for concerts and live dramatic performances. A tourist information kiosk and accessible public restrooms are available.

➤Continue walking along the Boardwalk for 1 block to Norwegian Lady Plaza. The bronze statue there was given to the people of Virginia Beach by the people of Moss, Norway, to commemorate the tragic wreck of the Norwegian sailing ship *Dictator* in 1891. It is a replica of the ship's figurehead, which washed ashore after the wreck. Simultaneous ceremonies were held in 1962 to celebrate the erection of the statue in Virginia Beach and an exact duplicate in Moss. In addition to hosting various small festivals throughout the year, the park is the site of commemoration each April to honor those who perished in the wreck and to celebrate the sister-city relationship between Virginia Beach and Moss.

(Author's note: If you would like to extend this walk, you can continue north on the Boardwalk for about a mile to 38th Street. At 40th, turn and follow the Boardwalk back to the Norwegian Lady.)

➤If you are continuing this walk, turn and walk south on the Boardwalk to 24th Street.

➤Turn right onto 24th Street and walk across Atlantic Avenue. At the northeast corner of 24th and Pacific Avenue, look for a white brick building, which now houses a surf shop. It was one of the first fire stations in the resort.

➤Turn left onto Pacific and walk 1 block.

➤Turn left onto 23rd Street to see Tautogs Restaurant, housed in historic Winston Cottage. You can almost imagine vacationers sitting in rocking chairs on the porch of this shingled cottage in the 1920s. The seafood served in the restaurant is some of the best on the beach, and the decor features a bar built with the original doors from rooms inside the cottage.

➤Return to Pacific and turn left.

The Old Coast Guard Station, now a maritime-history museum, was built in 1903 to help rescue sailors in peril. PHOTO COURTESY OF OLD COAST GUARD STATION

➤Walk 1 block to 22nd Street.

➤Turn right onto 22nd. In this block, you will see several fine examples of beach-cottage construction from the 1920s to the 1940s. The house at No. 310 was built in the Colonial Revival style; No. 314 exemplifies the Dutch Colonial Revival; and Nos. 304, 306, and 308 are typical bungalows or cottages.

➤Walk 5 blocks and turn right onto Parks Avenue. Enter the grounds of the Contemporary Art Center of Virginia. The museum exhibits an eclectic array of 20th-century art that is always changing and always fascinating. Exhibits range from mini-golf holes designed by contemporary artists to tile floors with holograms of faces looking up to neon sculptures that simulate rain. A small gift shop features unique gifts. Several fine pieces of contemporary sculpture can be found on the beautifully landscaped grounds.

➤Return to Parks and cross 22nd Street. The visitor information center on Parks can provide a wealth of information about Virginia Beach and surrounding cities. Accessible restroom facilities are available.

➤Cross 21st Street on Parks and turn right onto the grounds of the Pavilion Convention Center, which features a variety of trade and consumer shows, as well as musical entertainment in the theater.

➤Turn left onto the sidewalk adjacent to the building.

➤Turn right at the end of the building and walk toward the entrance drive. Before turning to leave the Pavilion parking lot, look right into the courtyard. *Light Garden* is an amazing example of contemporary sculpture featuring light-sensitive panels that change color as the daylight changes.

➤Walk down the entrance drive to 19th Street. Across the street is the Tidewater Veterans Memorial.

of interest

Tidewater Veterans Memorial

This monument was dedicated in 1988 to the service and sacrifice of thousands of American military men and women. Flags in the plaza represent all branches of the military and each city in the area. The divided columns represent "a world divided by war." The voids in the columns symbolize all that is lost when war takes place. The waterfall and the ever-filling pool unify the structure and represent "an effort to bring all people together." A small, landscaped park behind the monument is a place to reflect on the value of peace.

Virginia Beach and the Hampton Roads area have a long history of military presence. This monument resulted from a partnership of regional, private, and public interests who raised money for its design and construction.

➤Turn left onto 19th Street and return to Atlantic Avenue.

➤Turn right onto Atlantic Avenue. Visitors who have not been to Virginia Beach since the 1980s will notice a dramatic improvement in Atlantic Avenue. A recent $60 million facelift to the aging resort buried utilities, removed unsightly signs, and used decorative brick to pave sidewalks and side streets leading from Atlantic to the Boardwalk. Plants and sculptures ornament the streets. This beautification dramatically enhanced the appeal of the resort. Pacific Avenue is slated for renovation in the future.

➤Return to the 8th Street entrance to the parking garage.

The military has long played a role in the economy of the Virginia Beach area, and the Tidewater Veterans Memorial is one expression of the community's appreciation. PHOTO BY CAROLE J. ARNOLD

walk 2

Rudee Inlet

General location: Explore the southern end of the Virginia Beach Boardwalk and the commercial marine and residential areas surrounding Rudee Inlet.

Special attractions: Rudee Inlet, marinas, turn-of-the-century architecture.

Difficulty rating: Easy; flat, paved surface on sidewalk or roads.

Distance: 2 miles.

Estimated time: 1 hour.

Services: Restaurants and outdoor cafes on the Boardwalk and the inlet, portable public restroom at 2nd Street, water fountains along the Boardwalk.

Restrictions: Pets are not allowed on the Boardwalk or on adjacent grassy areas from May through September. From

Rudee Inlet

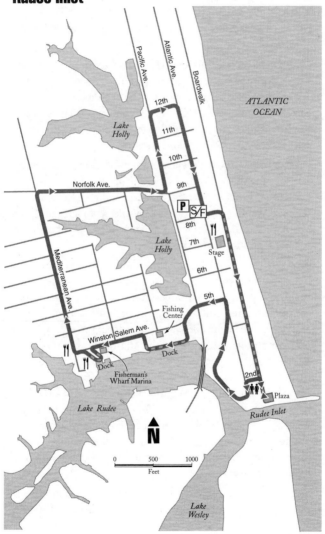

October through April, pets must be leashed and all droppings picked up.

For more information: Contact the Virginia Beach Visitor Information Center.

Getting started: Virginia Beach/Norfolk Expressway (Route 44) east provides access to the Virginia Beach oceanfront. As it enters the resort area, the expressway becomes 21st Street. Turn right onto Pacific Avenue and then left onto 9th Street, and enter the parking garage on your right. Parking fees vary depending on the season.

Public transportation: Tidewater Regional Transit Routes 20 and 24 provide access to the oceanfront from the west and end at the corner of 19th Street and Pacific Avenue. Transfer to Route 37 going south or walk 10 blocks south to begin this walk. Contact Tidwater Regional Transit for schedule and fare information.

Overview: At the south end of the Virginia Beach resort and hotel area, known as "The Strip," you will find a wide, sandy beach enjoyed year-round by surfers, strollers, anglers, and sun seekers. Sea gulls and brown pelicans soar overhead, and dolphins play in the waves from spring to fall. Spend a few minutes at the plaza on the end of the Boardwalk at Rudee Inlet, and you will see all kinds of watercraft returning from the ocean. Fishing boats, dive boats, personal watercraft, and pleasure boats use this passage from the safe harbor in Lake Rudee to the Atlantic. Sand accumulates rapidly in Rudee Inlet and must be constantly dredged to provide safe passage. Maintaining the inlet is vital to the tourism industry and to those who own homes along the inland waterways.

Plans call for the Boardwalk to be extended along the inlet and under the Rudee Inlet bridge, through the area known as "The Loop." This would connect it with the marinas and restaurants west of the resort.

As you leave the marinas, you will walk through Shadowlawn, an old neighborhood that remains popular with both young and old because of its proximity to the beach and the large shade trees for which it is named.

The walk

➤Leave the parking garage by the stairway in the southeast corner. You will emerge at the corner of 8th Street and Atlantic Avenue. Cross Atlantic Avenue. Notice the white frame structure on the corner, an unusual site amid the modern hotels. This turn-of-the-century structure was a servant's quarters for one of the large cottages that originally lined the oceanfront.

➤Carefully cross the bike path and turn right onto the Boardwalk. You will pass a small stage at 7th Street. There is nightly entertainment here during the summer and on weekends in spring and fall. Locals and visitors enjoy Mahi Mah's and Chick's, the two cafes next to the stage. The sculptures of sea turtles, beach balls, sandcastles, and fish were part of a renovation project to improve Atlantic Avenue and side streets leading to it. As you walk south along the shoreline, the black discharge pipe that you may see is a part of the Rudee Inlet dredging operation.

➤Walk to the plaza at the end of the Boardwalk.

➤Turn around at the end of the Boardwalk and return to 2nd Street. You can watch or take part in some of the best surfing in the city at this spot. The area next to the rock jetty is one of several unrestricted surfing areas in the city. For safety reasons, during the summer surfing is

of interest

Beach Erosion Control and Hurricane Protection Project

When you reach the beach at 8th Street, you will see the Beach Erosion Control and Hurricane Protection Project. The City of Virginia Beach and the U.S. Army Corps of Engineers initiated this $103 million project to protect the hotels, restaurants, shops, and homes along the beachfront and the street renovations, sculptures, and landscaping that were installed in the area in the 1990s. The project includes a new seawall from Rudee Inlet to 58th Street, renovation of the Boardwalk from Rudee Inlet to 40th Street, enhancement of the dunes from 58th Street to Fort Story, and widening of the beach along the project area. The project is expected to take several years.

This flood-protection project is one of only half a dozen such projects in the United States. It is designed to protect against storms of a strength occurring only about once every century. The seawall is made of steel encased in concrete. It incorporates a drainage system to pump storm water out to sea.

In addition to its protective value, the project includes architectural improvements such as plazas and decorative handrails. The stage at 7th Street was built in conjunction with the project, and many of the cafes along the Boardwalk were spruced up or expanded by private owners as a result of it. Look for the project logo with its waves and hurricane symbol. It was designed by a high school graphic-arts student. A student's design also inspired the pattern of bluefish and sea turtles that you can see on the face of the seawall.

A well-maintained sportfishing fleet awaits anglers looking for action in Rudee Inlet, at the south end of Virginia Beach.
PHOTO COURTESY OF VIRGINIA BEACH CONVENTION AND VISITOR DEVELOPMENT

only allowed early in the morning and late in the afternoon at other locations. The 1st Street area often gets the best waves as a result of sand accumulation around the jetty. It is the site of several surfing contests.

The annual East Coast Surfing Championship in August is the East Coast's oldest such event. With the largest surfing purse on the East Coast, it attracts close to 500 professional and amateur surfers from around the country. The contest includes events for men and women, body-boarding events, a bikini contest, and a concert by a nationally known recording artist. A surfing area on the south side of the jetty can also be seen from here.

➤Turn left onto 2nd Street and walk 1 block.

➤Turn left onto Atlantic Avenue and walk on the sidewalk around the Loop. The large steel arch you see is the

Rudee Inlet

In the 1960s, the city enlarged and dredged what was formerly a shallow marshy inlet and lined it with hundreds of 4- to 12-ton rocks to create Rudee Inlet. The stones were brought in by railroad and then carried by trucks to the beach. Cranes were used to lower them into place.

Virginia Beach is one of only a few municipalities in the country that owns and operates its own dredge. *The Rudee Inlet II*—the white, red, and blue dredge visible in the inlet or docked on the other side—is a hydraulic, cutter-suction dredge. It uses a blade system to cut into the sand and then suck it off the bottom of the inlet. The sand is pumped across the beach, and bulldozers spread it several blocks to the north along the shore. You may see a dark mixture of sand, saltwater, decayed leaves, and other natural materials flowing from the pipe. In a matter of days, the sun will bleach it.

Dredging Rudee Inlet is a constant battle for the *Rudee Inlet II*. Sand migrates from the south as a result of prevailing winds and currents, and waves push sand into the inlet. Sediment from the watershed surrounding Lake Rudee and Lake Wesley, which lie behind the inlet, also accumulates on the bottom. The U.S. Army Corps of Engineers helps maintain the inlet. Several times each year, a large corps dredge travels to Virginia Beach and dredges an area at the mouth that the *Rudee Inlet II* cannot reach. Deep-water access through the inlet is vital to charter fishing, whale- and dolphin-watching tours, scuba diving, and other water sports.

Skycoaster, a thrill ride that operates in the summer. Across the inlet you can see Croatan, an upscale beachfront community.

➤Turn left onto 5th Street.

➤Cross Pacific Avenue to Winston Salem Avenue.

➤After you pass the entrance to a condominium parking lot, turn left into the parking lot of the Virginia Beach Fishing Center. Look for the 1,093-pound blue marlin in the glass case near the marina store. Caught in 1978, this marlin holds the state record.

➤Turn right and walk along the wooden docks. The Fishing Center is one of three commercial marinas on Rudee Inlet. Its berths are occupied by sport and commercial fishing boats and by commercial and recreational dive boats. "Head boats," so-called because you pay "by the head," take anglers out into the ocean to fish the shallow waters for sea bass and other fish. The commercial fishing boats bring in large catches of sea bass, trout, and other food fish. The sportfishing fleet takes charters offshore as far as 90 miles to fishing holes—with names like the Cigar, the Hot Dog, the Humps, and the Lumps—to catch billfish such as blue marlin or game fish such as tuna and dolphin.

Walking along the docks, you will pass a fish-weighing station where anglers weigh large game fish and have souvenir pictures taken. If you time your walk for around 4 P.M. in the summer, you will see the charter boat fleet and the head boats returning with their catches.

➤Turn right at the end of the dock and return to Winston Salem Avenue.

➤Turn left and continue along Winston Salem to the Fisherman's Wharf Marina.

➤Turn left and walk along the floating docks. You will see the pleasure craft that permanently dock in Rudee Inlet or that stop briefly as they travel up and down the coast. Lobster pots occasionally clutter the docks. Commercial lobster operations in this area are sparse because lobster live in deep, cold water far offshore.

Lake Rudee, the body of water you see on your left, was dredged in the 1950s to rebuild the eroded beach. Across the water, you can see retaining walls and masonry supports. These bulkheads and revetments protect the earth embankments from the eroding power of rainfall and the ebb and flow of the tide. The opening of the inlet and the dredging of the basin spurred development as builders raced to provide homes and businesses with access to the ocean. Some parts of this basin are 35 feet deep as a result of the dredging. This waterway leads to the Owls Creek Salt Marsh Preserve and the Virginia Marine Science Museum (see walk 4).

➤Return to Winston Salem Avenue from the docks and turn left onto it. A third commercial marina at Rudee's Restaurant is a popular docking spot for diners who come to the inlet by boat for dinner.

➤Turn right onto Mediterranean Avenue. Since there are no sidewalks along Mediterranean, please use extra caution and walk facing traffic. This is a popular area for walking and biking, and most drivers use caution.

➤Walk along Mediterranean through Shadowlawn, one of the most popular neighborhoods in Virginia Beach. Close to the ocean and affordable, the neighborhood is a mixture of small, older beach cottages and new and renovated homes. The tall pines, hardwoods, and large flowering shrubs give the neighborhood an ambiance that newer neighborhoods struggle to achieve.

➤Turn right onto Norfolk Avenue and walk 3 blocks. At the corner of Pacific Avenue, you will see Lake Holly on your right and left. When the resort area developed, Lake Holly was a tidal marsh crossed in several places by pedestrian bridges from the beach to the residential area. A dam was built in 1890 to direct and control the tidal flow of water into the Lake Holly system. By maintaining a mixture of salt and fresh water in Lake Holly, city engineers found they could control mosquitoes and also provide saltwater fishing. The operation of the dam was a popular attraction as large quantities of water rushed out of the flume.

➤Turn left onto Pacific and walk 3 blocks to the intersection with 12th Street. Traces of the turn-of-the-century neighborhood remain in houses like the one on the northeast corner and the small cottages surrounding it. The hipped roof, dormers, and wraparound porch on the large house were typical of cottages in the young resort community.

➤Turn right onto 12th Street and walk 1 block to Atlantic Avenue.

➤Turn right onto Atlantic. As you walk south to return to the parking garage, at No. 1005 you will see another example of a servant's quarters from the early part of the 20th century.

➤Complete your walk at the 8th Street entrance to the parking garage.

walk 3

The North End

General location: This walk meanders through beachfront neighborhoods at "the North End" of Virginia Beach and along the Atlantic Ocean.

Special attractions: Beach cottages dating from the early 1900s, Greystone Manor (a recent addition to the National Register of Historic Places), the Association for Research and Enlightenment, historic Cavalier on the Hill Hotel, and a $103 million seawall project.

Difficulty rating: Moderate; flat, hard surfaces, except for approximately 1 mile on sandy beach.

Distance: 6 miles, with a 4-mile option.

Estimated time: 3 hours.

Services: Restaurants in both the new and old Cavalier Hotels and the Ramada Plaza Resort, guided tours of the

Association for Research and Enlightenment, tours of the Cavalier on the Hill.

Restrictions: Dogs are not allowed on the beach from Memorial Day weekend through Labor Day weekend, except before 10 A.M. and after 6 P.M. Pets must be leashed and all droppings picked up. On-street parking is limited; pay attention to all parking signs, even if they look unofficial. No public restrooms on this route.

For more information: Contact the Association for Research and Enlightenment or the Cavalier Hotels.

Getting started: The North End walk begins at the Cavalier on the Hill. To reach the hotel, take Virginia Beach/Norfolk Expressway (Route 44) east to the oceanfront. Route 44 becomes 21st Street as it enters the resort area. Turn left onto Pacific Avenue. The Cavalier on the Hill is on the west side of Pacific Avenue at 42nd Street. Pacific Avenue becomes Atlantic Avenue as you head north from this point. If you intend to tour the hotel, park at the hotel. Parking is available but limited on 42nd Street and other numbered streets. It is easier to find a spot in the early morning or late afternoon during the summer.

Public transportation: Tidewater Regional Transit Routes 20, 24, and 33 travel north along Atlantic Avenue with a stop at the two Cavalier Hotels. Contact Tidewater Regional Transit for schedule and fare information.

Overview: The North End, as locals call the neighborhoods in the northeastern corner of the city, is one of the most prestigious addresses in Virginia Beach. Residents have fiercely protected the area from commercialization. Many families have lived there for generations. Some of the homes in the North End are second homes for wealthy families and individuals from the state capital in Richmond or other cities around Virginia Beach.

The North End

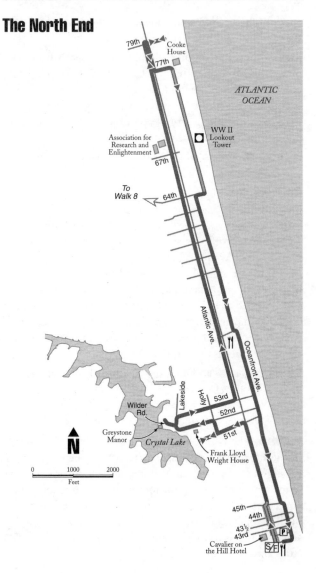

The neighborhood's eclectic character results from the juxtaposition of quaint cedar-shake cottages, some dating from the early part of the 20th century, to modern stucco beach mansions. Giant live oak trees and pines dominate the landscaping, and the sound of waves breaking on the beach in many places drowns out the noise of cars passing just beyond the oleander hedges.

The Association for Research and Enlightenment—a mecca to some and a mystery to others—draws thousands of visitors each year to study the life and work of the world-famous teacher and psychic Edgar Cayce. If you are interested in holistic health, dreams, reincarnation, ESP, meditation, or personal spirituality, you may want to add some time to this walk to more fully explore the association facility.

During the second half of the walk, you will follow the beach for approximately 1 mile. Since it is easiest to walk the beach at low tide, you may want to check the tide chart in the local newspaper to determine prime walking time. A hat and a dose of sunscreen are appropriate on any walk but especially this one during peak sun months. The beauty of the beach in any season and the spectacle of million-dollar beach houses make the beach portion of this walk unforgettable.

The walk

➤Begin the walk at the Cavalier on the Hill. This historic hotel towers over the beach resort and symbolizes the spirit of warm, Southern hospitality for which Virginia Beach has long been known.

Cavalier on the Hill

The Cavalier on the Hill dates from the mid-1920s, when approximately 100 investors hatched a plan to build a luxury hotel in what was then the small seaside community of Virginia Beach. With $2 million raised by the sale of public stock, they built the grand hotel. In time, it would host seven presidents and such celebrities as Judy Garland, Johnny Weismuller, Jean Harlow, Bob Hope, F. Scott Fitzgerald, and Sam Snead.

Guests arrived at the Cavalier on the Hill in limousines or in Pullman coaches from New York and Washington. The hotel's amenities included a seawater pool that was thought to be medically beneficial, accommodations for gentlemen's hunting dogs, a golf course modeled after St. Andrews in Scotland, sunken gardens, and an on-site stockbroker's office with a ticker tape feed directly from the New York Stock Exchange. Special spigots brought iced water from barrels on the roof. Guests at the opulent hotel dressed in gowns and tuxedos for dinner in the Pocahontas Room. The famous big bands from the 1930s, 1940s, and 1950s—including those led by Glenn Miller and Benny Goodman, who played in the hotel's beach club—helped to boost the hotel's reputation.

During the 1940s, the hotel became the site of a navy radar training school. It was eventually returned to service as a hotel, and today it continues the tradition of hospitality that it established over its 70-year history. Tours of the hotel are available on a limited basis and are worth the time. Be sure to look for the tiny "library," and ask if the tour can include the bell tower. The hammock under the live oaks near Atlantic Avenue can be a welcome respite for weary walkers.

The Cavalier on the Hill, a hotel built in the 1920s, epitomizes the spirit of warm, Southern hospitality for which Virginia Beach has long been known. PHOTO BY KATHERINE JACKSON

➤Leave the hotel on the north side and walk down the circular driveway to a brick path that leads between two brick walls. This quaint and quiet walkway offers a special peek at the North End lifestyle. The front doors of beach cottages and comfortable Colonial-style homes open onto the walkway, which is flanked by gardens filled with roses, magnolias, and camellias.

➤Cross several streets and access alleyways until you come to the end of the brick path then turn right onto 45th Street.

➤Cross Myrtle Avenue and take a left onto the walkway and bike path that parallels Atlantic Avenue.

➤Walk 6 blocks along Atlantic, a popular promenade for walking, in-line skating, running, and bicycling.

➤Turn left onto 51st Street and walk westward, away from the ocean. Several blocks back at the end of 51st Street, a gravel drive lined with bamboo leads to one of the three Frank Lloyd Wright houses in Virginia.

➤Return along 51st Street for 1 block and turn left onto Holly Road. On the northeast corner of the intersection of Holly and 52nd Streets is an unusual example of a 1920s beach home built of cinder block and stucco.

of interest

Frank Lloyd Wright House

World-renowned architect Frank Lloyd Wright designed the house at 320 51st Street with the living areas built in a crescent. Completed in 1959, the house is adjacent to Crystal Lake and, as with all Wright's signature designs, it integrates indoor and outdoor living spaces with the wooded, waterfront environment.

The sand-colored brick exterior is broken by narrow windows in the sleeping wing and French doors in the living wing. Radiant heat is embedded in the cast-concrete floors, and built-in furnishings take advantage of interior spaces. Half-walls, especially in some of the small rooms in the sleeping area, create the feeling of spaces larger than they measure.

The house is occasionally open for tours. Contact the Virginia Beach–Princess Anne Historical Society for more information.

➤Turn left onto 52nd Street. This part of the neighborhood is interesting in that, even though you are only a few blocks from the oceanfront, you get the feeling of a mature and stable suburban neighborhood. Some local residents think 52nd Street is the prettiest street in Virginia Beach, with its mature pines and tended lawns. As you walk westward, you will catch a glimpse of Crystal Lake, a small body of water that provides deep-water access through Broad Bay and Chesapeake Bay to the ocean.

➤At the end of 52nd Street, turn right onto Lakeside Avenue.

➤Turn left immediately onto Wilder Road. In the middle of the street, a California redwood welcomes visitors to Greystone Manor, formerly known as Lakeside.

➤Walk back down Wilder and turn left onto Lakeside Avenue. Walk 1 block.

➤Turn right onto 53rd Street. An interesting aspect of the North End is its eclectic combination of architectural styles. You will see charming cottages next to rambling ranches and towering mansions. The homes display diverse building materials—from cedar shakes to brick to vinyl siding. The proximity of North End property to the ocean guarantees its resale value no matter what kind of structure occupies it.

➤Turn left at the feeder road, a secondary walking and bicycling access road that parallels Atlantic Avenue, and continue north to the Association for Research and Enlightenment at 67th Street.

Automobile traffic entering and exiting Atlantic frequently crosses this path, so be careful at all intersections. If you turn left onto 64th Street, you reach the start of the Narrows walk (see walk 8).

of interest

Greystone Manor

Designed in the Scottish Baronial style, this home at 515 Wilder Road was built by Dr. John Miller-Masury and his wife, Martha Miller. It took two years to complete the building of the 12,000-square-foot mansion. Blue Vermont granite, green Pennsylvania slate, and other building materials were brought in by rail.

The framework of the house was made of Douglas-fir imported from the Pacific Northwest, the flooring of local oak, and the paneling of Brazilian mahogany. These touches, along with ornate plaster ceilings, made the mansion unique in its day. Seven fireplaces augmented the heating system, which was powered by a generator that also operated an elevator and electric lights. The three-story structure contained 25 rooms, a grand ballroom, and 3,000 square feet of verandahs and sunporches. Every window has a view of Crystal Lake.

The 184-acre estate included windmills, a steam boiler, fruit orchards, and stables. A boardwalk led past the California redwood, that Miller-Masury planted as a reminder of his second home in California, to an oceanfront gazebo half a mile away. The mansion's remote building site gave it the feeling in its early years of being out in the "wilderness."

Lakeside provided a longtime home for Miller-Masury, a doctor who trained at Columbia Medical School, the heir to a paint-manufacturing fortune, and a master mariner. In 1935, a North Carolina business group renamed the house the Crystal Club and operated it as a gambling casino and nightclub. Also known at one time or another as Masury Manor, the Castle, and the Wilder Place, the mansion reverted to a private residence following World War II. Through the years, the estate was subdivided and the sale of lots became the genesis of the North End neighborhood. The house is on the National Register of Historic Places. It is privately owned and occupied.

Association for Research and Enlightenment

The Association for Research and Enlightenment, founded in 1931 and located at the intersection of Atlantic Avenue and 67th Street, attracts thousands of visitors from around the world to study the life and work of Edgar Cayce. Described as an average man—husband, father, photographer, and Sunday school teacher—Cayce became famous for his professed psychic abilities. While in a self-induced trance, he would provide answers to questions and respond to diverse discourses. These were collected and promoted as his "readings."

Initially, Cayce's subject matter revolved around physical ailments and remedies associated with mind-body relationships. As a result, he has been called "the father of holistic medicine." He eventually expanded his realm of knowledge to include subjects such as world religions, philosophy, psychology, dreams, history, the life of Jesus, ancient civilizations, soul growth, psychic development, reincarnation, and prophecy.

The association visitor center offers guided and taped tours, lectures, workshops, video presentations, discussion groups, a bookstore, and a library that includes Cayce's 14,000 readings and other materials on topics such as holistic health and comparative religions. Sixty thousand volumes on parapsychology comprise one of the largest such collections in the world. A gallery displays descriptions of Cayce's research. A meditation room on the third floor overlooks the ocean, and the prayer and meditation garden on the west end of the center provides a quiet spot for reading or contemplation.

The white building that parallels Atlantic Avenue was built in the late 1920s and originally housed the Edgar Cayce Hospital. It now serves as the organizational headquarters.

(Author's note: If you would like to shorten this walk to 4 miles, head south to 63rd Street. Turn left and cross Atlantic Avenue. Turn to page 54, where you will pick up the walk at the corner of 63rd Street and Oceanfront Avenue.)

➤Continue north along Atlantic Avenue and note the residential neighborhood replete with live oaks that have withstood time, northeasters, and occasional hurricane-force winds. Live oak trees are short, thick-trunked evergreen trees whose leaves have a waxy coating that protects them from salt spray and hot sun. Notice how many of them lean to the southwest as a result of strong winds from the northeast.

➤At 79th Street, cross Atlantic. At No. 107, you will see an example of the two-story houses that were commonly built in rural areas at the turn of the 20th century. With the addition of shingled walls, they also were popular as beach cottages.

➤Recross Atlantic to the parallel feeder road and turn left to head south.

➤At 77th Street, turn left at the stoplight. Note the gigantic, old live oaks that stretch halfway across the street. At the end of the street, the Cooke House sits beside the entrance to a public beach. Walk along the boardwalk toward the ocean for a wonderful view of the magnificent house.

The Cooke House is one of the few remaining examples in Virginia Beach of an early-20th-century oceanfront cottage. A rare survivor of a once-common type of architecture, it presides in stately fashion over the wide dunes. Its cedar-shingled exterior, hipped roof with dormers, brick chimneys, and verandahs on three sides evoke images of seaside days gone by, of bonfires on the beach and women in bathing costumes gathering at low tide. The view across the wide North End sand dunes and sea grass is spectacular.

Access to public beaches is available at the east end of most numbered streets. The access ways may be boardwalks, cement walkways, or sandy trails. Seashells, horseshoe crabs, and shards of colored glass sanded smooth by the ocean await beachcombers on Virginia Beach. If you are a dedicated seeker, you may occasionally find sand dollars and sea stars. You are more likely to find seaweed, bits of coral, and clamshells. Watch for ghost crabs darting along the shoreline, dolphins feeding or playing just off the coast, and flocks of pelicans soaring overhead. For more information on the marine environment, take the Owls Creek Salt Marsh walk (walk 4), which includes a stop at the Virginia Marine Science Museum.

Although many beaches in the country are continually eroding, the beach at the North End continues to grow. Sand from beach replenishment projects at the south end migrates to the north. Beach grass and sea oats shoot root-stems under the sand, and new plants grow out of the nodes on the roots. Sand collects around the base of the plants, helping the dunes to grow and stabilize.

➤Turn right onto the beach and head south for 14 blocks, or approximately a mile, to 63rd Street.

➤Turn right onto the beach access path at 63rd Street. The path is approximately 20 houses south of the wooden lookout tower—a leftover from World War II—at Officer's Club Beach at 67th Street.

➤At the end of the beach access, turn left onto Oceanfront Avenue, one of the most charming lanes in Virginia Beach.

If you miss 63rd Street, you can use any of the access ways to the south to get to Oceanfront Avenue. If you get to the Ramada Plaza Resort at 57th Street, you will know you have gone too far. You can still get onto Oceanfront via the beach access at 57th Street.

(Author's note: If you chose to shorten this walk, resume following the directions here.)

At the corner of 63rd and Oceanfront is a classic beach cottage covered in shingles, trimmed in white, and landscaped with live oaks, holly trees, and fragrant Russian olive bushes. This house, as well as the Cooke House on 77th, was identified as a historically significant example of early 20th-century cottage design. This house has maintained its large lot, which is unusual in the North End, where every foot of space is creatively worked into the pleasant patchwork that gives the neighborhood its character.

➤Continue along Oceanfront to 58th Street. The white brick house on the corner at No. 101 is also noted for its historic significance.

➤Make a quick left turn onto 58th and then turn right to continue on Oceanfront. Notice the cedar-sided house on the corner at No. 4501.

➤Turn left at 44th Street and walk down to the beach. From there, you will be able to see evidence of the Beach Erosion Control and Hurricane Protection Project, which provided a seawall from Rudee Inlet to 58th Street, an improved boardwalk at the south end of the beach, and an enhanced beach and dune system along the entire oceanfront to 89th Street. The seawall's primary purpose is to protect the beach from storms, but it features a bas-relief pattern of sea turtles, bluefish, and waves making it decorative as well.

➤Return to Oceanfront, knock the sand out of your shoes, and turn left. Continue walking to 42nd Street.

➤Turn right onto 42nd and walk 1 block to Atlantic Avenue.

➤Turn left onto Atlantic and walk to the traffic light for one last, spectacular view of the Cavalier on the Hill, Virginia Beach's grandest old lady. You have completed your tour of the North End.

walk **4**

Owls Creek Salt Marsh

General location: South of Rudee Inlet. The Owls Creek Nature Trail, which leads through woods and a salt marsh, is part of the Virginia Marine Science Museum.

Special attractions: Animal habitat, 30-foot observation tower, aviary, marine science museum.

Difficulty rating: Easy; flat, on paved, wooden, or hard-packed dirt surfaces.

Distance: 1 mile.

Estimated time: 45 minutes.

Services: Restaurant, wheelchair-accessible restrooms, gift shops.

Restrictions: Pets are not allowed.

For more information: Contact the Virginia Marine Science Museum.

Owls Creek Salt Marsh

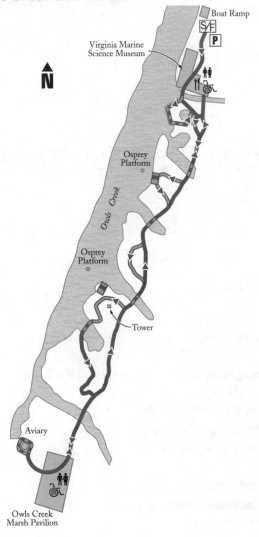

Getting started: This walk begins in the parking lot of the Virginia Marine Science Museum. To reach the museum, travel east on Virginia Beach/Norfolk Expressway (Route 44). Turn right onto Pacific Avenue. When you cross the Rudee Inlet bridge, Pacific becomes General Booth Boulevard. The museum is on General Booth, about half a mile beyond the bridge on the right. Park at the back of the lot near the boat ramp.

Public transportation: Tidewater Regional Transit Route 37 provides access to the museum. From June through August, the Museum Express Trolley runs from the hotels in the resort area to the museum. Contact Tidewater Regional Transit for schedule and fare information.

Overview: The Virginia Marine Science Museum is one of the top-ten marine science and aquarium facilities in the country. The mission of the museum is to educate visitors about marine life in and around Virginia waters. Exhibits and aquariums feature information on and examples of the fish, birds, and plants that live in the Owls Creek Salt Marsh, on which the museum is located, and in the Atlantic Ocean, into which the creek flows. The museum also has exhibits on freshwater coastal rivers and Chesapeake Bay. A nature trail joins the main museum building with the Owls Creek Marsh Pavilion. You may want to spend time exploring the main museum and the pavilion to learn about the living exhibit you will see outdoors. Interpretive display boards and volunteers stationed along the trail provide additional information.

Highlights of the museum include a shark tank, a seaturtle aquarium, and a "touch tank" where you can pet live stingrays. An IMAX theater features three-dimensional science and nature films. Scheduled programs and volunteers in red shirts elaborate on the exhibits. Listen for announcements of special programs.

After you complete this educational walk, you can eat lunch or a snack on an open-air deck that looks out onto the salt marsh. The museum shops offer unique gifts and educational materials relating to the marine environment.

The walk

➤Begin near the boat ramp adjacent to the museum parking lot.

➤Walk toward the museum on the sidewalk that parallels the water until you come to an observation deck. The forested property across Owls Creek was dedicated in 1992 as the navy's first Watchable Wildlife Area in Virginia. This property and property owned by the museum make up the Owls Creek Salt Marsh Preserve. Many of the tulip poplars and loblolly pine trees you see along the shoreline are more than 100 years old.

➤Continue toward the museum via the sidewalk.

➤Walk around the harbor-seal aquarium and in the front entrance of the museum to the admissions desk.

➤Turn right after leaving the admissions desk to enter the exhibit area.

➤Turn right again and look for the sign indicating the way to the salt marsh trail.

➤Turn left into the Salt Marsh Room as you pass a display of carved-wood bird decoys.

➤Leave the building through the doors on your left. On the deck to your left is a field-guide sign that describes the plants in the adjacent wildflower garden. Depending on the season, you can see Indian blanket flowers, Carolina jasmine, Queen Anne's lace, black-eyed susans, tickseed sunflowers, asters, daisies, and other flowers.

of interest

Owls Creek Salt Marsh

The 100-acre Owls Creek Salt Marsh is directly connected to the Atlantic Ocean. These wetlands serve as a food source and habitat for marine animals. They also filter pollution from rainwater runoff and prevent erosion. Owls Creek is highly saline because of its proximity to the Atlantic Ocean and the tidal inflow of saltwater.

More than 10,000 species of plants and animals inhabit the salt marsh at various times of year. Some animals frequent the marsh during their annual migrations. Others, such as terns, visit the area in spring and fall, when food is abundant. Many fish raise their young among the protective marsh grasses. Nine species of heron are among the most visible animals in the marsh. It is also the northernmost habitat of the brown pelican and the southernmost range of the common loon. Opossums and white-tailed deer frequent the forested wetlands, and barracuda and lookdown fish travel to the creek from the ocean. River otters, once an endangered species in Virginia, hunt and fish the creek and its banks.

➤Follow the boardwalk into the salt marsh.

➤Turn right at the first intersection and follow the signs to the loop trail. Another field-guide sign on the observation deck provides information on egrets, blue herons, mergansers, mallards, barn swallows, and other birds that live in the area. Use the binoculars mounted on the deck to spot wildlife.

➤Continue along the boardwalk until you reach the next observation deck, where a field-guide sign describes the tidal system and the shrimp, periwinkle, crabs, insects, and mussels living in these waters and on the tidal flats.

Boardwalks and observation decks allow visitors to the Virginia Marine Science Museum a unique perspective on life in the Owls Creek Salt Marsh. PHOTO COURTESY OF VIRGINIA MARINE SCIENCE MUSEUM

➤Follow the boardwalk until you cross a small freshwater pond. Look for the yellow-bellied slider turtles gliding through the water in search of food.

➤Turn right at the next intersection and cross the marsh via the wooden bridge. Is anyone home in the birdhouse on the right?

➤Turn right onto a hard-packed dirt path to the observation deck. A field-guide sign contains a tide clock so that you can determine the current point in the tidal cycle. The platform you see across the water was built as a nesting site for ospreys.

➤Turn right when you reach the paved trail. Cross the bridge into the woods.

➤Turn right onto the hard-packed dirt trail. You are now following the Meadows Loop Trail. Meadow plants grow

of interest

Ospreys on Owls Creek

The populations of ospreys and other raptors here were once decimated by the widespread use of DDT and other insecticides. Pesticide-polluted rainwater drained into the marsh and affected the fish. These were eaten by the birds, which developed reproductive problems as a result. Since the institution of a ban on these pesticides, the osprey has been making a slow comeback.

Also called a fish hawk, the osprey is a large bird with a white head, a wingspan of 5 feet, and angled wings. Its plumage is dark above and white below. When it spots a fish, the osprey folds its wings and dives toward the water. As it nears the surface, it slows, extends its talons, and grabs its prey. It may even dive under the surface. Like many anglers, the osprey often comes up without a fish.

Ospreys build large nests of sticks, branches, and beach debris. Each year, mating pairs return to nests they used the previous year and add more sticks. These nests can weigh up to 1,000 pounds—as much as a small car! Ospreys mate for life and can live as long as 20 years.

in sunny clearings in the forest. Look for the butterflies, birds, and mammals that feed on nectar, seeds, and leaves found in the meadow.

➤Continue walking toward the paved trail and turn right onto it.

➤Cross the bridge and turn right toward the Watchable Wildlife Deck. On the left is a simulated osprey nest. Climb the 30-foot observation tower or use the monitor at the base of the tower to get a bird's-eye view of the marsh and the osprey platform across the creek.

➤Walk to your right and turn right when the path forks. The boardwalk leads to another wildlife observation deck. Notice the animal tracks carved into the wooden planks. Signs identify these as belonging to deer, otters, herons, and raccoons.

You are now in the Coastal Woodland Retreat, where you will learn about the trees growing in this forest. Open the exhibit boxes to see displays about the barks and leaves of white oak, American beech, loblolly pine, yellow poplar, red maple, and other trees. Take a minute to close your eyes and listen to the songbirds that fly in and out of the trees.

➤Turn right at the intersection and notice the small signs placed in the ground to identify plants native to the area.

➤Turn right and cross the wooden bridge over the marsh. On your right is the aviary.

➤Walk toward the Owls Creek Marsh Pavilion and notice the river otter exhibit on your right.

➤Walk through the doors and pass the river otter viewing area. This building features interactive exhibits and a movie depicting life in the salt marsh.

➤Turn right and pass through the doors to walk around the aviary. Unlike many aviaries, which contain exotic birds, this one features only North American birds. More than 50 species live in this netted exhibit. Binoculars tethered to the railing of the boardwalk allow you to get a closer look. All the permanent residents of the aviary are injured or otherwise incapable of surviving in the wild. However, the songbirds you see can fly in and out through the netting. A field-guide sign to the birds is displayed on the deck. Knowledgeable volunteers point out the herons and egrets, ducks, gulls, woodpeckers, pelicans, and vultures that live in the trees and pools of the aviary.

➤Leave the aviary and retrace your steps through the pavilion to return to the nature trail.

➤Cross the wooden bridge and take the center path at the intersection.

➤Stay on the main path as it winds its way back to the main building of the museum. See how many trees, flowers, birds, and animals you can now identify in the forest and marsh.

➤As you reach the final loop of the trail, stay to the right to reenter the museum.

➤Return to the parking lot to complete your adventure in the salt marsh.

walk 5

First Landing and First Lighthouse

General location: On the northeastern corner of the city, this walk surveys the area around Cape Henry at the mouth of Chesapeake Bay.

Special attractions: Two lighthouses, First Landing Cross, ocean and bay views.

Difficulty rating: Easy, but lighthouse has stairs.

Distance: 1 mile.

Estimated time: 45 minutes.

Services: A small market provides refreshments and restrooms.

6 4

First Landing and First Lighthouse

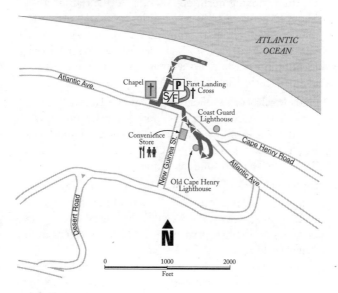

Restrictions: Pets must be leashed and all droppings picked up. Parking is restricted to marked parking lots. Observe all "Official Business/Off Limits" and "Restricted/Occupants and Guests Only" signs. Dunes are off limits. $1 fee to climb to top of lighthouse.

For more information: Contact the Association for the Preservation of Virginia Antiquities or the Fort Story public affairs office.

Getting started: Fort Story, a U.S. Army base, is at the northern end of Virginia Beach. Take the Virginia Beach/Norfolk Expressway (Route 44) to Pacific Avenue. Route 44 becomes 21st Street as you enter the resort area. Turn left onto Pacific Avenue. Pacific becomes Atlantic Avenue at the traffic light in front of the Cavalier on the Hill Hotel. Continue driving north on Atlantic. At the traffic light at Shore Drive, turn right and continue driving north a few more blocks until you pass through the Fort Story gate, which is usually not staffed. If it is staffed, you may be asked to show identification such as a driver's license. Drive into the base and park at the First Landing Memorial Site parking lot.

Public transportation: Tidewater Regional Transit Route 24 serves Fort Story. From points west, Route 20 provides service to the oceanfront. Transfer at 19th where Route 24 can be taken north to Fort Story. Contact Tidewater Regional Transit for schedule and fare information.

Overview: Named for a son of King James of England, Cape Henry has become known as the site of the "first landing" of English settlers in the New World. Those settlers went on to found the first permanent English settlement in the New World at Jamestown, Virginia.

The area became an army installation in 1914, when the Virginia General Assembly gave the land to the federal government for military use. Fort Story was named for Virginia-born General John Patton Story, one of the most noted coastal artillerymen of his day. It has served as a training ground and as the site of a convalescent hospital. In 1946, the mission of the fort changed when it became the site of army amphibious training. It also provides space for U.S. Navy explosive ordnance training and Marine Corps amphibious and landing training.

After your walk, you can visit the public beach by crossing the parking lot near the entrance gate. This undeveloped stretch of beach is a perfect place to spend an afternoon with a picnic or a good book.

of interest

The First Landing Cross

English settlers erected the First Landing Cross on or near this spot in 1607, after sailing to the New World aboard the *Susan Constant*, *Godspeed*, and *Discovery*. Captain George Percy's account of the landing describes "fair meadows and goodly tall trees, with such fresh waters running through the woods as I was almost ravished at the first sight thereof." When 28 men disembarked to explore the area, Chesapeake Indians attacked them. The next day, a second group landed without incident. On the third day, the members took a small boat upriver as far as present-day Hampton. On the fourth day, they set up a cross and dubbed this spot Cape Henry. The party sailed up Chesapeake Bay and the James River to establish the first permanent English settlement in the New World at Jamestown. In 1935, the large stone cross that stands today was placed on the site to commemorate this first landing.

The walk

➤Begin your walk at the south end of the parking lot of the First Landing Memorial Site. Beyond a sign that tells about the history of the area, cross the grassy field toward the First Landing Cross.

➤Cross the lawn to another stone monument that features a diagram of a French and British naval engagement that took place off the Virginia capes during the Revolutionary War. General George Washington had asked the French to help him set up a blockade around Yorktown to prevent supplies from reaching British troops there. Admiral François

Joseph Paul de Grasse responded and defeated the British fleet in the Battle Off the Capes. The monument has quotes from Washington and de Grasse expressing their appreciation for the cooperation.

➤Continue walking toward the statue of Admiral de Grasse. Turn right onto the boardwalk leading to the top of the dunes. From this vantage, you can see the site of the sea battle. To your left, you will see the bridges of the Chesapeake Bay Bridge-Tunnel. You can also see huge commercial barges and naval ships that are serviced at the region's ports and shipyards.

Acclaimed one of the seven wonders of the modern world, the 17.6-mile Chesapeake Bay Bridge-Tunnel crosses the bay from Cape Henry at Virginia Beach to Cape Charles on Virginia's Eastern Shore. It consists of 12 miles of trestle and road; two tunnels, each a mile long; two bridges; two miles of causeway; and four manmade islands. It is one of the world's largest bridge complexes. The toll route cost $200 million and took more than three years to build, opening on April 15, 1964. It cuts 95 miles off the route from Virginia Beach to New York. The bridges are ideal places from which to watch for birds, and rare coastal birds have been spotted there.

➤Return to the parking lot, turn right, and walk along the sidewalk. On your right is St. Theresa Chapel, surrounded by holly trees. A statue set into the brick and stone facade and a carved wooden door adorn the small chapel. A picnic table on the north side provides a quiet resting spot.

➤Return along the sidewalk and cross the parking lot.

➤Cross the street to walk along the sidewalk heading toward the lighthouse.

➤Turn right into the parking lot and enter the small visitor center. In the plaza at the base of the lighthouse, you can

This 150-foot-tall cast-iron lighthouse, built in 1881, is considered the tallest fully enclosed lighthouse in the nation.
PHOTO BY CAROLE J. ARNOLD

use binoculars to view the ocean and bay. Keep an eye out for dolphins, which are frequently seen where the bay meets the ocean.

➤Climb to the top of the lighthouse for an exceptional view of the cape, First Landing/Seashore State Park, the bay, and the ocean.

➤Return to the parking lot at the memorial site to complete your walk.

of interest

Old Cape Henry Lighthouse

In 1792, the federal government built its first lighthouse at the mouth of Chesapeake Bay on land donated by the state of Virginia. It was one of the first official acts of President George Washington. Known as Cape Henry Lighthouse, the structure was constructed of stone from the Aquia Quarries near Alexandria, Virginia, which also provided stone for the White House, the U.S. Capitol, and Mount Vernon.

Thirty feet in diameter, the lighthouse rises to a height of 72 feet. Oil lamps were used to provide the light until 1812, when an Argand lamp with reflectors replaced them. During the Civil War, the lighthouse was attacked; after the war, it was deemed unsafe and was closed. It is now listed on the National Register of Historic Places.

The 150-foot cast-iron lighthouse adjacent to Old Cape Henry Lighthouse was completed in 1881. Now operated by the U.S. Coast Guard, it is considered the tallest fully enclosed lighthouse in the nation.

walk 6

Bald Cypress Trail

General location: A trail through an untouched forest just a few blocks from the Atlantic Ocean in the northeastern corner of the city.

Special attractions: Maritime forest, cypress lagoons, animal and bird habitats.

Difficulty rating: Moderate; sandy path through forested sand dunes and cypress swamps.

Distance: 1.5 miles.

Estimated time: 1 hour.

Services: Visitor center, wheelchair-accessible restrooms, drinking water only at the visitor center.

Restrictions: Pets must be leashed at all times. Park hours are 8 A.M. to dusk. Bicycling is only allowed on the Cape Henry Trail.

For more information: Contact First Landing/Seashore State Park and Natural Area.

Getting started: This walk begins at the First Landing/Seashore State Park Visitor Center. Take Virginia Beach/Norfolk Expressway (Route 44) to the oceanfront. Route 44 becomes 21st Street. Turn left onto Pacific Avenue, which becomes Atlantic Avenue at the traffic light in front of the Cavalier on the Hill Hotel. Atlantic curves around to Shore Drive. Turn left at the traffic light into the park. You must pay a parking fee, except Wednesdays, when parking is free.

Public transportation: None.

Overview: First Landing/Seashore State Park is an ecological jewel in the midst of the heavily populated northern part of Virginia Beach. Almost 20 miles of trails wind through 2,800 acres of maritime forest, bayfront beaches, and cypress swamps that contain 500 species of plants. A small visitor center includes exhibits on the geological history, plants, and animals of the area. Other amenities include campsites, rustic cabins, a picnic area, and a boat ramp.

Cape Henry, the corner of land where the Atlantic Ocean meets Chesapeake Bay and where the park is located, was formed 3,000 to 5,000 years ago. Much of the forest in the park looks today as it did in 1607, when sailors from the English ships *Susan Constant*, *Discovery*, and *Godspeed* landed here. In 1770, the governor of Virginia designated land west of the cape, including that which would become the park, as a "Common for Benefit of the Inhabitants of the Colony in General for Fisheries and Other Public Uses." The land, often referred to as "the Desert" in those days because it was uninhabited, remained a common until it was sold to an unsuccessful lumbering operation. It was resold to a syndicate of businessmen who in turn sold it to the Commonwealth of Virginia.

Seashore State Park opened in 1936 after 600 members of the Civilian Conservation Corps spent six months building the trails and roads. The park was eventually renamed First Landing State Park to commemorate the 1607 landing of the settlers who eventually established the first permanent English settlement in the New World at Jamestown.

The Bald Cypress Trail is a moderately difficult 1.5-mile loop through the woods and cypress swamps. It is an interesting introduction to the landscape and to the plant and animal life in the park. The trail is marked with red blazes. At the visitor center, an interpretative brochure is available for 50 cents, and a checklist of plant and animal life is available for $2. Rain can turn the trail muddy in spots.

The walk

(See map on page 78.)

➤Leave the visitor center by the back door and follow the boardwalk across the lagoon and into the climax forest. Be careful on all boardwalks because the planks can be slippery when damp.

➤Turn left at the end of the boardwalk and follow the red arrows that denote the Bald Cypress Trail. Notice the smells and sounds of the park as well as its sights.

➤Turn right and follow the boardwalk into the middle of the cypress lagoon. Keep an eye out for turtles sitting on logs. This park is the only place in Virginia known to support the chicken turtle, which has a neck nearly as long as its shell. Flier, perch, and blue-spotted sunfish are also found in these swamps.

of interest

The bald cypress lagoon

First Landing/Seashore State Park is filled with bald cypress trees and lagoons. Bald cypresses differ from other cypresses in that they lose their leaves every fall. Notice the wooden "knees" on the tree trunks where they protrude from the water. Scientists are unsure of their purpose. Some believe they help the trees breathe. Others believe they provide added support.

The water in these lagoons is fresh. Pirates and explorers were thankful to find it because it contains a high level of tannin, a natural acid found in leaves and wood that helped to keep the water fresh during long voyages. The stains on the tree trunks indicate the fluctuations in the water level.

The gray Spanish moss that hangs from trees is a rootless plant that thrives on air and rain. Unlike parasites, which take nutrients from the trees, this moss does not harm its hosts. The park is at the northern edge of the range for Spanish moss, and the plant is on the state endangered-species list. Remember not to disturb the moss or any other plants or animals.

Succession, which takes thousands of years to occur, happens in the lagoon as leaves and dead trees fall into the water and rot. The layer of peat they form fills in the swamp and becomes fertile soil in which plants begin to grow. A mature forest eventually replaces the lagoon.

The Chesapeake Indians, one of the Algonquin tribes, lived farther inland where the land was better for farming. However, they hunted and fished in this area because of the abundance of fish, deer, and shellfish such as oysters, clams, and mussels.

Who lives in the park?

Because of its proximity to the Atlantic Ocean and the Gulf Stream, the southeast corner of Virginia has a moderate climate that supports many species of plants and animals not typically found in other parts of the state or farther north. Examples include Spanish moss, sea oats, live oak, the southern cricket frog, the chicken turtle, and the short-billed dowitcher.

More than 150 species of birds have been spotted in the park. Ospreys, or fish hawks, return to the park each spring. Their nests are often visible in the tops of trees adjacent to the water. This large fish-eater can be identified by the angled shape of its long wings and the white plumage on its underside. Cardinals, robins, warblers, and blue jays flit among the branches of the pines and beeches. Herons and egrets frequently stalk prey along the edges of the ponds, and belted kingfishers dive headfirst into the water in pursuit of fish. Gulls, ducks, and pelicans also flock to the water. The green heron is a small, dark bird with orange or yellow legs. The snowy egret has white plumage and a gracefully curved neck. Listen and look for red-headed woodpeckers, whose rectangular doorways mar the trunks of bald cypress trees. Although other species of woodpeckers have red feathers on their heads, the red-headed woodpecker is the only eastern woodpecker whose head is entirely red.

Holes in trees provide shelter for flying squirrels, bats, raccoons, and lizards. Gray foxes live in the area but are elusive and rarely seen. Snakes slither through the water and along the trails. Seventy species of trees have been identified in the park, including live oak, blackjack oak, American beech, loblolly pine, wax myrtle, and redbay.

➤Return to the trail and follow the path to the right when it intersects with the Osmanthus Trail. This 3.1-mile trail is named for the osmanthus, an evergreen wild olive tree that grows prolifically along it. The tree sports yellow and white blossoms in April and May. If you want to lengthen the Bald Cypress walk, you can take the Osmanthus Trail; it loops around and reconnects with the Bald Cypress Trail.

➤Continue along the Bald Cypress Trail, watching for the red blazes painted on trees. You are climbing and descending sand dunes that once fronted the shoreline. As sand accumulated on the beach, new dunes formed in front of these dunes. Shrubs and small trees replaced the beach plants. The swales between the dunes became swamps as rainwater drained into them, and succession continued until a mature forest was formed.

➤Cross the Cape Henry Trail and follow the red arrow to continue on the Bald Cypress Trail. A right turn on Cape Henry will take you back to the visitor center. Close your eyes and tune your ears to the forest sounds, including the voices of frogs, songbirds, and woodpeckers. The spring peeper, whose call sounds like sleigh bells, is commonly heard in this area.

➤Continue along the Bald Cypress Trail when you reach its intersection with the High Dune Trail—or explore the High Dune Trail. The High Dune's highest point is not far from this intersection, and it is a steep slope. Since it is heavily forested, the peak does not provide a panoramic view. On the Bald Cypress Trail, you will pass wooden stairs coming down from the Fox Run Trail.

➤Turn left when you reach the Cape Henry Trail again for the short walk back to the visitor center. If you prefer to continue walking, you can turn right and take the Broad Bay walk (see walk 7).

walk 7

Broad Bay

General location: Explore an untouched forest and the shores of Broad Bay in the northeastern corner of the city.

Special attractions: Maritime forest, cypress lagoons, 65-foot sand dunes, tidal bay, wildlife.

Difficulty rating: Difficult; sandy path through the forest and cypress swamps; high dune ascents.

Distance: 6 miles.

Estimated time: 4.5 hours.

Services: Visitor center, wheelchair-accessible restrooms, drinking water only at the visitor center.

Restrictions: Pets must be leashed at all times. Park hours are 8 A.M. to dusk. Bicycling is only allowed on the Cape

Broad Bay

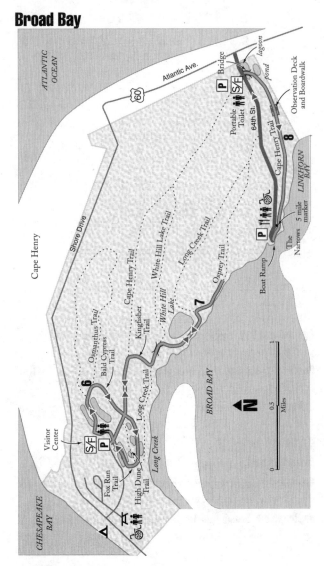

Henry Trail. The Long Creek and Osprey Trails can be impassable at high tide or during times of heavy rain. You may have to wade through ankle-deep water. Inquire about the condition of the trail at the visitor center.

For more information: Contact First Landing/Seashore State Park and Natural Area.

Getting started: This walk begins at the First Landing/Seashore State Park Visitor Center. Take Virginia Beach/Norfolk Expressway (Route 44) to the oceanfront. Route 44 becomes 21st Street as it enters the resort area. Turn left onto Pacific Avenue. Pacific becomes Atlantic Avenue farther north, at the traffic light in front of the Cavalier on the Hill Hotel. Atlantic curves around to Shore Drive. Turn left at the traffic light into the park. You must pay a parking fee, except on Wednesdays, when parking is free.

Public transportation: None.

Overview: The Broad Bay walk takes you on several trails that provide an extensive view of the natural amenities of the park—from its untouched cypress swamps to its forested dunes and the shores of Broad Bay. Along the route, you will pass White Hill Lake, a pristine body of water where you may see an egret or an osprey. If you enjoy solitude, you may well find it on this trail. A guide to the plants and animals in the park is available at the visitor center.

the walk

(See map on page 78.)

➤The walk begins in the corner of the parking lot across from the visitor center. Walk between two signs that read "Unleashed Pets and Motor Vehicles Prohibited."

➤Turn left onto the Cape Henry Trail. A short wooden observation walk on the right provides a view of the swamp, with its cypress "knees" and Spanish moss.

➤Continue past the 1-mile marker. The Cape Henry Trail is 5 miles long and is the only trail in the park where bicycling is allowed.

➤Turn right onto the Kingfisher Trail and pass through the opening in the wooden fence. Marked by white signs and tree blazes, the Kingfisher Trail is 0.6-mile long and shaded by a canopy of American beech trees. You can identify the beech by its green and gray dappled trunk and elliptical leaves.

At the end of the Kingfisher Trail, you will crest a small hill. Here you will get your first view of expansive Broad Bay in the distance.

➤Turn left onto the Long Creek Trail and enjoy the expansive view of Broad Bay and the adjacent marshlands.

Broad Bay is a tidal bay and one of a series of inland bodies of water. The bay eventually joins the Lynnhaven River, which empties into Chesapeake Bay. Broad Bay is a popular summer recreation area for boaters, sailboarders, canoeists, and personal-watercraft users, as well as a habitat for diverse animals and fish. The waterfront homes visible across the bay are some of the most desirable in the city because of their access to the ocean and their views of the park.

➤Turn right when you reach a clearing in the woods, and cross a concrete bridge to continue on the Long Creek Trail, which is marked with orange blazes. (If you continue going straight, you will walk 1.5 miles along the White Hill Lake Trail to the Cape Henry Trail.) Notice the oysters and fiddler crabs clinging to the bridge.

➤Continue to follow the Long Creek Trail as it descends

of interest

A pirate treasure

The pirate Edward Teach became known as Blackbeard because of his vanity about his extravagant facial hair, which he often festooned with ribbons. In the early 18th century, Blackbeard led a band of pirates who ambushed and looted merchant ships that traveled along the Virginia and North Carolina coasts carrying goods and money between Europe and the American colonies. The inland waterways adjacent to Chesapeake Bay were a perfect hiding place to wait for unsuspecting mariners.

According to local legend, Blackbeard buried treasure at a place called Blackbeard's Hill, which is probably located within the park. He was reportedly hunted down and killed before he was able to retrieve his loot. Perhaps, if you are lucky, you will find a trace of the buccaneer's booty.

toward White Hill Lake. As the trail follows the lakeshore, look for osprey nests in the tops of the trees.

➤Climb the trail up a steep sand dune. As you walk along this ridge of sand, you will have several spectacular views of Broad Bay. At 65 feet, these dunes comprise the highest natural point in Virginia Beach. The tall buildings visible in the distance are condominiums on the shore of Chesapeake Bay. Continue walking along the ridge and through the mossy forest.

➤When you come to the intersection of the Osprey and Long Creek Trails, take the Osprey Trail. A large yellow sign at the intersection warns that the Osprey Trail may flood at high tide. Go down the steep slope, using the make-shift wooden stairs.

➤Walk along the shore of the bay. Be careful as you cross the washed-out bridge or ford the shallow stream. You may be walking in ankle-deep water.

Relax on the beach and enjoy the sights and sounds of the bay. The Broad Bay walk concludes when the trail returns to the forest. If you prefer to continue on the Osprey Trail, it will intersect after approximately 1 mile with the Long Creek Trail, which leads back to White Hill Lake. This loop will add approximately 2.5 miles to the Broad Bay walk.

➤Turn around and retrace your path along the Osprey Trail, which is marked with green blazes, to the Long Creek Trail, which is marked with orange blazes.

➤Turn left onto the Long Creek Trail.

➤Follow the Long Creek Trail to the Kingfisher Trail, which is marked with white blazes.

➤Turn right onto the Kingfisher Trail and retrace it to the Cape Henry Trail.

➤Turn left onto the Cape Henry Trail and return to the visitor center.

First Landing/
Seashore State Park

walk 8

The Narrows

General location: Explore an untouched forest and the shores of Linkhorn Bay in the northeastern corner of the city.

Special attractions: Maritime forest, cypress lagoons, tidal bay, boat launch, wildlife.

Difficulty rating: Moderate; sandy path through the forest and cypress swamps.

Distance: 3.5 miles.

Estimated time: 2 hours.

Services: Wheelchair-accessible restrooms, portable toilets, water at each end of the trail, seasonal concession stand.

Restrictions: Pets must be leashed at all times. Park hours 8 A.M. to dusk. Bicycling allowed only on the Cape Henry Trail.

For more information: Contact First Landing/Seashore State Park and Natural Area.

Getting started: This walk begins at the First Landing/Seashore State Park parking lot on 64th Street. Take Virginia Beach/Norfolk Expressway (Route 44) east to the oceanfront. Route 44 becomes 21st Street as it enters the resort. Turn left onto Pacific Avenue, which becomes Atlantic Avenue at the traffic light in front of the Cavalier on the Hill Hotel. From Atlantic, turn left onto 64th Street and enter the park. Park in the small lot on the right side of the road. If this lot is full, follow the road through the park to the parking lot at the other end of the trail and do this walk in reverse. You must pay a parking fee, except on Wednesdays, when parking is free.

Public transportation: Tidewater Regional Transit Routes 24 and 33 provide access along Atlantic Avenue to 64th Street. Route 20 provides access nights, weekends, and holidays. Contact Tidewater Regional Transit for schedule and fare information.

Overview: This walk is along a portion of the Cape Henry Trail, the most heavily traveled trail in the park. The Cape Henry Trail leads from the visitor center off Shore Drive to the Narrows, a distance of 5 miles one-way.

The walk to the Narrows follows the Cape Henry Trail for just over 1.5 miles from the parking lot on 64th Street. The trail rolls gently up and down sandy hills and beside several bodies of water. This trail exemplifies the variety of the landscape in the park, from exotic cypress lagoons to the forested dunes and sandy bayshore. If you are vigilant, you may spot an osprey fishing or an egret stalking its prey. This peaceful walk is a favorite in all seasons because the tree canopy provides protection from winter winds and summer sun.

the walk

(See map on page 78.)

➤Leave the parking lot and cross 64th Street.

➤Walk over the cypress swamp via the wooden bridge. Look for the bald cypress trees, which thrive in water up to their "knees." This area is occasionally flooded during heavy rains. If the bridge is impassable, turn right on the road and walk approximately 0.1 mile until you see several cylindrical pilings in the ground on the left side. Turn left here and walk between the pilings to access the trail.

➤Pass the 3.5-mile marker. This trail is part of the 5-mile route from the visitor center to the Narrows.

➤At the first fork, turn right and traverse several sandy hills. During the spring, this path is lined with dogwood trees in bloom. Fall is a colorful time as the deciduous trees turn from green to red and gold.

➤Walk past the pond and watch for birds that either live in the park year-round or rest in the park during migration.

➤Cross the marsh via the boardwalk. The small observation deck is an excellent place to watch for ospreys in the spring and summer. You can see their nests in the tops of dead trees. Ospreys are large birds with angled wings, white heads, and white breasts. They are fish-eaters and find the park to be a bountiful source of food. Marshes like this one were once considered undesirable swamps, but we now realize the value of tidal wetlands as habitat for wildlife and as filters of polluted rainwater.

After you cross the marsh, you will begin to glimpse Linkhorn Bay on your left.

➤Go to your left when you reach the 5-mile marker at the end of the trail.

➤Walk toward the "staircase" made from wood pilings. To the left, just before the staircase, is a sign that depicts the waterways in this area and how they flow toward the ocean.

➤Ascend the stairs for a panoramic view of the Narrows and Broad Bay. This popular recreation area draws thousands of visitors each year. The boat launch just beyond the sandy hill is one of only a few public boat ramps in the city.

➤Cross the dune and walk down the hill to your right to the boat-ramp parking lot.

➤Walk through the parking lot to begin the return trip via the park access road. Use caution and walk on the side of the road facing traffic. You may choose instead to return via the Cape Henry Trail. About a mile down the road, you will see the end of the Osprey Trail, which would lead you to the Broad Bay walk (walk 7).

of interest

The inland waters

The Narrows is a shallow body of water connecting Linkhorn Bay and Broad Bay, both of which are part of the Lynnhaven River system. The Lynnhaven flows into Chesapeake Bay, which leads to the Atlantic Ocean. When early English colonists arrived, there was probably an inlet at what is now the intersection of 48th Street and Atlantic Avenue. A hurricane or other major storm likely caused the inlet, which connected Linkhorn Bay with the ocean, to fill. Early settlers described Lynnhaven oysters as large and delicious, and in the early 1900s these shellfish were internationally renowned. The channel through the Narrows is dredged to keep the area accessible for boating. The dredged sand is placed on the dune you see.

As you walk along the road, notice where the roots of trees have pressed up through the asphalt. Listen to the song-birds and enjoy the tranquility of this oasis in the middle of a busy city.

➤Return to the parking lot to complete your walk.

walk 9

The Courthouse

General location: Explore the Virginia Beach Municipal Center in a walk that includes new and historic government buildings.

Special attractions: Historic courthouse, city hall, municipal buildings.

Difficulty rating: Easy; flat, and entirely on sidewalks.

Distance: 1.25 miles.

Estimated time: 45 minutes.

Services: Wheelchair-accessible restrooms at the Virginia Beach Public Information Office and restrooms and refreshments at several restaurants along the route.

Restrictions: Pets must be leashed and their droppings picked up.

For more information: Contact the Virginia Beach Public Information Office.

Getting started: This walk begins in the municipal parking lot at the intersection of North Landing Road and Courthouse Drive. From the Virginia Beach oceanfront, drive south on Pacific Avenue. After crossing the Rudee Inlet bridge, Pacific becomes General Booth Boulevard. Continue on General Booth until it becomes North Landing Road. Turn left into the parking lot at the intersection of North Landing and Courthouse Drive.

Public transportation: Tidewater Regional Transit provides service to the Virginia Beach Municipal Center on Route 39. Contact Tidewater Regional Transit for schedule and fare information.

Overview: The Virginia Beach Municipal Center may seem misplaced, since it is not near the commercial centers of the city. However, a look at a map shows that it is actually in the geographic heart of the city. When the town of Virginia Beach and Princess Anne County merged in 1963 to become the City of Virginia Beach, the neighborhood of the historic Princess Anne County Courthouse was chosen as the center of city government. Many people still refer to this area as "The Courthouse." The city hall, judicial center, city jail, police headquarters, and public-school administration building are located in this pleasant rural setting. The public information office, which you pass on this walk, is a good place to stop for information on events and activities around the city. Most public buildings are open from 8:30 A.M. to 5 P.M. on weekdays.

The architecture of the historic courthouse, which opened in 1824, set the tone for the entire municipal center. The courthouse has been significantly altered over the years, but

The Courthouse

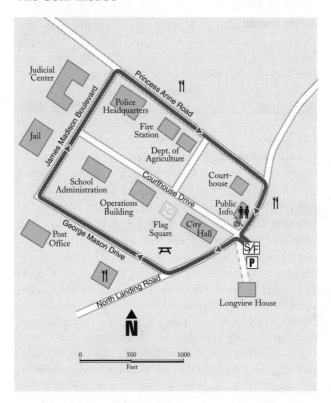

its colonial style and red brick facade are reflected in the surrounding buildings, many of which were built in the 1960s.

The municipal center hosts a variety of activities during the workweek. Its stately buildings and manicured lawns also provide a pleasant setting for weekend walks. Restaurants here bustle with municipal employees Monday through Friday but offer a quiet refuge on weekends.

the walk

➤Walk out of the parking lot along the same road you drove in on. When the stand of trees on your left ends, look back along the dirt driveway to see 206-year-old Longview House.

of interest

Longview and its ghost

When Longview was built in 1793, the construction date was etched onto a brick in the chimney. The original house had only one room below and two small rooms above. As the fortunes of the owners improved, they enlarged and improved the house. The original clapboard exterior was eventually replaced with brick, laid in the Flemish style. The City of Virginia Beach purchased the house in 1987. Although it is privately occupied, the house and its grounds will one day become a part of the growing public complex that surrounds them.

The ghost of a Confederate soldier is said to inhabit the house. James Howard Whitehurst, a relative of the former owners, was wounded in the Battle of New Market and returned to Princess Anne County to live out his final years. Residents have told many stories of his continued presence.

Blossoming Bradford pear trees bracket the red-brick tower of City Hall, a fairly modern building constructed to reflect the city's colonial roots. PHOTO BY CAROLE J. ARNOLD

➤Cross North Landing and turn left. On your right is Virginia Beach City Hall, which opened in 1969. This red brick, colonial-style building houses the city manager's office and city council chambers. The council-manager form of government was adopted in 1963, when the city and county merged. The city council is comprised of 11 elected officials, including a popularly elected mayor, and is charged with setting policy and giving direction to the city manager, who runs the day-to-day operations of the government. City council meetings are open to the public and are held the first, second, and fourth Tuesdays of each month. Contact the Virginia Beach Public Information Office for a schedule if you are interested in watching local government in action.

➤Turn right onto George Mason Drive. On your left you will pass Brewer's East, a popular lunch spot for municipal employees. As you look to your right, you will see Flag Square, where the flags of the United States, Commonwealth of Virginia, and City of Virginia Beach fly.

As you continue along George Mason, you will pass the city operations building and the school administration building on the right. Be sure to notice the variety of trees, shrubs, and flowers in the municipal center. The Bradford pear trees that line this street and others make a glorious display when their white flowers bloom in the spring.

➤Turn right at the stop sign onto James Madison Boulevard. The building on the left is the city jail, which was designed in the same colonial style as the other municipal center buildings. The building has windows, but the cells do not. The crape myrtle trees that line this street bloom in summer.

The Virginia Beach Judicial Center is the next group of three buildings on your left. These buildings house offices

Princess Anne Courthouse

The Princess Anne Courthouse was the sixth such facility to serve Princess Anne County, which was carved in 1691 from neighboring Lower Norfolk County. The building site was chosen because it was in the geographic center, though not the population center, of the county. Previous courthouses had been located closer to Chesapeake Bay and the early settlements in that vicinity. In 1824, when the courthouse and jail were constructed at this spot known as "The Cross Roads," a commercial district and village began to grow around them. The area became a trading center for surrounding farms.

Over the years, the jail and several other buildings were torn down and replaced. Only the original courthouse remains, though it has been so heavily renovated that it was denied status as a state historic landmark. Its colonial style and Flemish-bond brick became the model on which the remainder of the buildings in the municipal complex were designed. The building continues to serve as offices for municipal operations, but all court services are now housed in three buildings at the new judicial center on the other side of the municipal center. The statue of a Confederate soldier in front of the courthouse was designed by Charles Walsh and donated in 1905 by the Daughters of the Confederacy.

Today, the area around the municipal center continues to grow and attract businesses and residential development. It may one day be the population center of the city as well as the center of government.

that support the operation of the circuit court, general district court, and juvenile and domestic relations court. Opened in July 1995, the complex includes space for nine more courtrooms as the city grows. The court buildings are open to the public.

➤Turn right onto Princess Anne Road, where a magnolia tree grows on the corner. On your right is police headquarters. In front of the building, you will see a memorial square with three stones listing the names of Virginia Beach police, fire, and rescue officers killed in the line of duty.

Continue walking past the Courthouse Fire Station and the Department of Agriculture. Virginia Beach is the most populous city in the Commonwealth of Virginia, yet its agricultural community still thrives. There are more than 150 farms inside the city limits, with approximately 33,000 acres of land under cultivation.

➤Walk to the corner of North Landing and Princess Anne. The residential area to your left has been designated a historic district to control development. This portion of North Landing is heavily traveled and not safe to negotiate on foot.

➤Turn right onto North Landing and pass the historic courthouse on your right. The public information office is housed in the next building on your right.

➤Turn left into the parking lot to complete your walk.

walk 10

Farmer's Market

General location: The walk starts at Princess Anne Park and the Virginia Beach Farmer's Market, which are located near the geographic center of the city in what was originally Princess Anne County.

Special attractions: Wooded park, amphitheater, Farmer's Market.

Difficulty rating: Easy; paved sidewalks with traffic crossing lights and accessibility for people with disabilities.

Distance: 2 miles.

Estimated time: 1 hour.

Services: Wheelchair-accessible restrooms, picnic shelters, two restaurants, Farmer's Market, special events.

Restrictions: Pets must be kept on a short leash and all droppings picked up. The park is open from 7 A.M. until sunset.

For more information: To reserve picnic shelters or get information on events at Princess Anne Park, contact the Virginia Beach Parks Leisure Events office. For information on market events, contact the Virginia Beach Farmer's Market.

Getting started: This walk begins in the parking lot at Princess Anne Park. From Virginia Beach/Norfolk Expressway (Route 44), take Exit 3A (Independence Boulevard/Princess Anne Road). When the road forks, veer right to stay on South Independence Boulevard. Turn left at Princess Anne Road and right onto Concert Drive to reach the parking lot.

Public transportation: Tidewater Regional Transit Routes 12, 29, 36, and 39 provide access to the Virginia Beach campus of Tidewater Community College, which is across the street from Princess Anne Park. You can get to the park from the oceanfront by taking Route 20 to the transfer point at First Colonial and Laskin Roads and transferring to Route 29. Contact Tidewater Regional Transit for schedule and fare information.

Overview: When the resort town of Virginia Beach merged with Princess Anne County in 1963 to become the City of Virginia Beach, this part of Princess Anne County became the geographic center of the city. Although best known as a resort community, Virginia Beach was historically an agricultural area. Today, the city economy includes significant commercial, agricultural, and military components. Here in the heart of the city, the agricultural heritage remains apparent, even though much of the farmland has been developed. To the south, approximately 33,000 acres of land comprise more than 150 working farms that produce everything from corn to hogs. Farmer's Market provides spaces for many of these farmers to sell their strawberries, peaches, blackberries, cantaloupes, tomatoes, corn, and other crops.

Farmer's Market

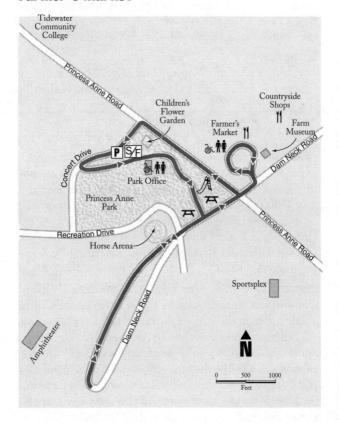

When a development company that owned much of the farmland in the area went bankrupt, Virginia Beach bought a vast tract of land for a bargain price. This property has rapidly become a hub of recreation and entertainment compared by many to Central Park in New York City. An amphitheater, a new PGA Tournament Players Club golf course, soccer and softball complexes, and a multipurpose sportsplex that is home to a professional soccer team and host to international competitions have recently been built near Princess Anne Park, which already boasted a horse arena and tennis courts. These amenities have both improved the quality of life in the city and bolstered tourism.

Future development will include the campus of a major university adjacent to the existing community college, the expansion of the Farmer's Market, and the construction of several public schools whose students can use the sports and educational opportunities nearby.

of interest

Princess Anne Park

In this 302-acre regional park at the edge of the urban area, you will find picnic shelters, volleyball nets, horseshoe pits, and softball and soccer fields. A 3,600-seat horse arena hosts equestrian events and rodeos. Each year, 288,000 people use the park for picnics and athletics. The annual Folk Arts Festival, held the first weekend in August, draws artists, crafters, and entertainers from around the country. The shady grove of pine and hardwood trees is a favorite spot for picnics. You can reserve a shelter through the Virginia Beach Parks Leisure Events office.

of interest

Farmer's Market

The Virginia Beach Farmer's Market opened at this location in 1976 and has provided a focal point for the city's agricultural industry for more than 20 years. Vendors sell everything from fruits and vegetables to honey, herbs, flowers, holiday wreaths, and other seasonal produce.

In addition, the market provides wholesome family entertainment rooted in rural traditions. During fair weather, Friday night hoedowns and country line dances attract people of all ages. An annual Country Fair Day includes a petting zoo and activities such as cow milking and barrel racing. You can often find crafters' fairs and flea markets here on weekends.

A community committee has recommended expanding the marketplace to include educational activities and exhibits, such as a demonstration farm plot and a tie-in with nearby Tidewater Community College.

Spend time walking around the Farmer's Market, and be sure to check out the shops behind the center ring and the truck vendors. Your visit will not be complete without a stop for ice cream at Bergey's Dairy Farm store. The Mennonite farm, located near the neighboring city of Chesapeake, produces ice cream and other products in an old-fashioned dairy.

the walk

➤Begin the walk in the parking lot at the Children's Flower Garden, where small flower beds are surrounded by holly, crape myrtle, and weeping willow trees. Children under six are invited to visit with an adult and pick flowers in season.

Vendors selling a cornucopia of fruits, vegetables, and other produce attract lookers and buyers alike to Farmer's Market at the city's center.
PHOTO BY CAROLE J. ARNOLD

The garden and its stone benches provide a respite at the end of this walk.

➤Turn left when you leave the garden and cross the parking lot toward the flagpole.

➤Cross in front of the park office and turn into the woods. Follow the paved walkway through the pines.

➤Turn right when you enter the small parking lot at the end of the paved walkway. Walk along the sidewalk on Dam Neck Road.

➤Cross Recreation Drive in front of the horse arena, where you can sometimes see the city's finest horses and riders practicing or competing in equestrian events.

➤Walk to the end of Dam Neck Road. Here you will see the GTE Virginia Beach Amphitheater, a 20,000-seat facility that opened in 1996. Each summer, the facility hosts approximately 40 entertainers, including such renowned performers as Elton John, Tina Turner, and Jimmy Buffett. Beautifully landscaped with ponds, fountains, and trees, the amphitheater is the perfect setting for an evening of relaxation with family and friends.

➤Turn and retrace your path along Dam Neck Road. To the right, you will see the new Virginia Beach Sportsplex, where professional soccer matches and events such as the Amateur Athletics Union Junior Olympics are held.

➤Cross Princess Anne Road at the pedestrian signal and enter Farmer's Market. A small farm museum near the market sign features antique farm equipment and information on Virginia Beach's agricultural heritage and traditions. You may want to spend time browsing in the Countryside Shops or eating in the cafe.

➤Return to Dam Neck Road and turn right onto Princess Anne Road. Continue along Princess Anne Road until you reach the pedestrian crossing at Concert Drive.

➤Turn left onto Concert Drive and end your walk with a rest in the Children's Flower Garden at Princess Anne Park.

walk 11

Mount Trashmore Park

General location: Mount Trashmore Park is off Virginia Beach/Norfolk Expressway (Route 44), approximately 9 miles west of the oceanfront.

Special attractions: World-renowned landfill, lakes, wildlife, playground, skateboard park, Water-wise Landscaping Garden, special events such as concerts and movies.

Difficulty rating: Easy; flat, trails on pavement and dirt with some uneven surfaces. Stairs on the front side and a ramp on the backside provide access to the top of the hill, which is 68 feet above sea level.

Distance: 2 miles.

Estimated time: 1 hour.

Services: Picnic shelters, wheelchair-accessible restrooms, vending machines for snacks and sodas.

Restrictions: Pets must be leashed and all droppings picked up. The park is open from 7:30 A.M. until sunset.

For more information: Contact Mount Trashmore Park or the Virginia Beach Parks Leisure Events office. You can also reserve picnic shelters through the Leisure Events office.

Getting started: This walk begins at the Leisure Events office at Mount Trashmore Park. To reach the park, take Virginia Beach/Norfolk Expressway (Route 44) west from the oceanfront and use Exit 3A (Independence Boulevard/Princess Anne Road). After exiting the ramp, you will be on South Independence Boulevard. Turn left at the traffic light onto Edwin Drive and follow the street until you see the Leisure Events office building, where you can park.

Public transportation: Tidewater Regional Transit Routes 29, 36, 39, and 61 travel Independence Boulevard. If you get off at Edwin Drive, you will be approximately half a mile from the Mount Trashmore Park parking lot. From the oceanfront, use Route 20 and transfer at Corporation Lane to one of the routes listed above. Contact Tidewater Regional Transit for schedule and fare information.

Overview: Mount Trashmore Park was the first landfill park in the world. It was conceived during the 1960s, when ecological consciousness was increasing. Opened to the public in 1973, the park continues to bring international recognition to Virginia Beach, and it symbolizes citizens' commitment to environmental protection. Rising 68 feet above sea level, the landfill is the tallest point of land in the region. The park encompasses approximately 166 acres, 79 of which are covered by Lake Trashmore. This park is the city's most popular, with more than 800,000 visitors annually. Citizens have voted Mount Trashmore Park their favorite place to picnic and fly a kite and have named it the best park in the city.

Mount Trashmore Park

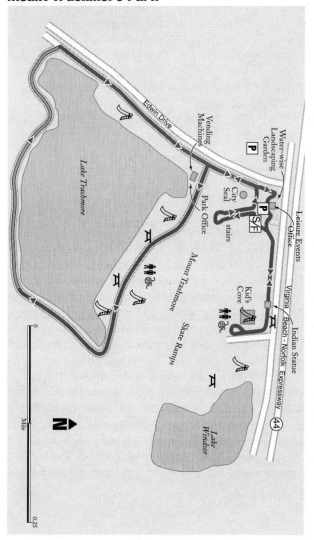

When conceived by Roland E. Dorer, who was director of the state Department of Health, Insect, and Vector Control, the project seemed an ideal solution to environmental, ecological, and sociological concerns. No one had ever tried building a mountain out of trash, but Dorer believed that piling trash and covering it, rather than burying it in an area with a high water table, would allow the landfill to hold more and last longer.

The Virginia Beach City Council approved the idea, and a demonstration project for the construction of the mound and amphitheater began. The effects of the landfill on subsoil and groundwater were carefully monitored. Conveyor belts were used to move waste from central bins to the work site, where it was layered with soil. Seven years later, the landfill was full.

The success of the project has generated worldwide interest, and other cities have studied the system to see whether it will work for them. The U.S. Environmental Protection Agency has approved the project and authorized similar ones.

Lingering environmental concerns, including erosion of the lakeshore, water quality, and waterfowl management, have been addressed in a renovation plan. The design calls for new wetlands, new vegetative buffers, and educational centers.

The popularity and success of the park led to the construction of a second landfill park, a portion of which opened in 1998. When completed in 2015, the new mountain will be three times higher and six times wider than Mount Trashmore. Mount Trashmore Park and its new sister park are examples of solid-waste disposal methods that are ecologically sound and contribute to the recreational assets of the city.

of interest

Virginia Beach City Seal

Study the official Virginia Beach seal and you will learn what the community values. It incorporates symbols for the city's historic and natural resources, such as Cape Henry Lighthouse, the first lighthouse commissioned by the U.S. government. First Landing Cross was erected at Cape Henry in 1607 by the English settlers who continued up the James River to establish the first permanent English colony in the New World at Jamestown. The sun and sand depicted on the seal symbolize the tourist industry, which hosts 2.5 million visitors annually. Strawberry leaves in a circle around the outside stand for the importance of agriculture, and a ring of marlins symbolizes the sportfishing industry.

the walk

➤Begin at the Leisure Events office at the corner of Edwin Drive and South Boulevard. The landfill is directly in front of the building. A large city seal is depicted on the grassy slope.

➤Climb the stairs to the small observation area surrounded by evergreens at the top and you will be at the highest point in town.

➤Descend from the summit and turn left to walk through the parking lot. You will come to a paved walking path on your left.

➤Turn left onto the path and walk alongside the hill. You are approaching Lake Trashmore, home to hundreds of seagulls and ducks.

➤Turn left at the small park building. To the left is an amphitheater that comes to life on most mild weekends with family events, concerts, and movies. You are now on a path that leads approximately 1.25 miles around the lake.

➤Follow the path along the lakeshore. You can rest on one of the benches before continuing to the undeveloped area of the park.

➤Turn right as you pass two neighborhood walkways to the park and continue along the southern side of the lake. This area has been left undeveloped. The pathway is dirt or mulch, and native plants grow untended. The path runs along the edge of some woods, and trees partially obscure the lake.

➤Turn right when you come to the paved path next to Edwin Drive. Trees planted along the lake here illustrate why Virginia Beach has been named a Tree City USA for almost two decades. An aggressive citywide tree-planting program gives residents a chance to plant trees in memory of loved ones.

➤Continue walking past the playground and park office until you return to the parking lot at the Leisure Events office.

➤Cross the parking lot and take the brick path that leads through the Water-wise Landscaping Garden.

➤Leave the garden after you pass the Leisure Events office. Check the time on the sundial.

➤Cross the parking lot access road and continue along the paved path toward the giant bust of an Indian. It was sculpted by Peter Toth and dedicated to Native Americans on July 15, 1976, as part of the nation's bicentennial celebration. With a traditional feather headdress, the sculpture stands two stories tall among the wax myrtles.

of interest

Water-wise Landscaping Garden

The Water-wise Landscaping Garden was created in the early 1990s by the Virginia Beach Citizen Water Conservation Awareness Committee, with the help of local nurseries, greenhouses, and landscaping contractors. At the time, water use was restricted because the rapid growth of the city was overtaxing its limited water supply. Since outdoor watering is one of the largest uses of municipal water, the garden was conceived to show residents that landscaping can be beautiful without an abundance of water.

The garden demonstrates seven steps to water-wise landscaping: planning, design, soil preparation, limited turf areas, appropriate plant selection, use of mulches, and appropriate maintenance. The garden is divided into sections based on water needs. For example, Texas yucca and Chinese holly thrive in the low-water-use region. By using plants native to the area and properly planning and maintaining landscaping, residents can significantly reduce water consumption.

As a result of the garden and educational efforts that include water-wise landscaping contests, Virginia Beach residents are among the lowest consumers of water in the nation. Although a new water supply project has been constructed since the garden was built, water-wise landscaping remains popular.

Regardless of the time of year, the garden features a pleasing array of plants, including creeping phlox, maiden grass, wax myrtle, pampas grass, Hillspire juniper, and Eastern red cedar. The plants are identified with small signs. A brochure with plant names and water-wise landscaping techniques is available at the Leisure Events office.

Kid's Cove, a fairly recent addition to Mount Trashmore Park, was made possible through the cooperative effort of individuals and civic organizations. PHOTO BY CAROLE J. ARNOLD

➤Turn right after passing the statue and walk past Kid's Cove, a wooden play structure constructed in 1993 by the Virginia Beach Junior Women's League and other community organizations. Individuals and civic organizations donated all the equipment, and volunteers provided the skills to put the playground together. Residents purchased pickets to build the fence that encircles it. On the pickets are engraved names and sentiments, such as "Molly loves Ken," "Greaux Family," and "Blair and Brian Eason." Just beyond Kid's Cove is a skateboard park.

➤Retrace your steps to the Leisure Events office to end this walk.

walk 12

The Elizabeth River

General location: Located in the Kempsville area of the city, this walk meanders through the woods and along the banks of the Elizabeth River. It follows the Elizabeth River Nature Trail, which begins at Carolanne Farm Neighborhood Park.

Special attractions: Natural wildlife habitats, scenic river views.

Difficulty rating: Easy; flat, dirt path.

Distance: 1 mile.

Estimated time: 45 minutes.

Services: No water or restrooms on the trail or in the park.

Restrictions: Pets must be leashed and all droppings picked up. The trail can be muddy, especially after rain. Watch out for poison ivy. The park is open from sunrise until sunset.

The Elizabeth River

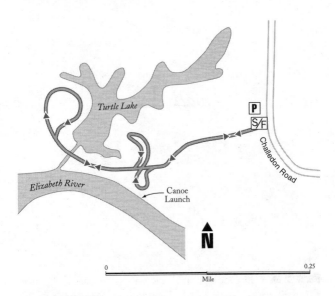

For more information: Contact the Department of Parks and Recreation. A nature guide to the walking and canoe trails is available at the Virginia Beach Central Library or the Kempsville Area Library. It includes a checklist of the plant and animal life seen from the trail.

Getting started: From the oceanfront, take Virginia Beach/ Norfolk Expressway (Route 44) west approximately 10 miles to the Witchduck Road exit. Turn left at the end of the exit ramp and travel south on Witchduck Road. Turn right onto Princess Anne Road. Turn left at the traffic light at Coventry Road and then right onto Challedon Drive. The park will be on the left. Park on the street, being careful not to block driveways.

Public transportation: Tidewater Regional Transit Route 39 traverses Princess Anne Road. The walk begins approximately 2 miles off Princess Anne. Contact Tidewater Regional Transit for schedule and fare information.

Overview: Smack in the middle of the most populated area of the city, this walk through the woods and along the eastern branch of the Elizabeth River will introduce you to a rich ecosystem brimming with freshwater and saltwater plants and animals. You may spot ducks, ospreys, peregrine falcons, herons, and songbirds, maybe even a gray fox or bald eagle. The woods and river teem with squirrels, rabbits, turtles, snakes, lizards, and frogs.

Chesapeake Indians once walked these woods and paddled canoes along this stretch of river. Early British and Spanish settlers explored the area around the turn of the 17th century and likely found the remains of Indian camps. The area was settled and named Kempsville after an early resident. The river provided a way to transport supplies to the settlers even though the water was only deep enough to navigate at high tide. Farms occupied this area until the 1980s, when it was acquired by the city for public use.

the walk

➤Walk straight down the short park road and onto the path that leads into the woods. On the right, notice where the tended lawn is being allowed to revert to nature. Grasses are the first plants to reestablish themselves after an area has been cultivated for farming, followed by shrubs and then pioneer trees, such as loblolly pines. This process is called succession.

Next, you will enter a young pine forest that was planted approximately 35 years ago. Later on the trail, you will pass through a climax forest—the culmination of the succession process. The pine forest is replete with shrubs and vines, including poison ivy and honeysuckle. On the right side of the trail, notice the forested wetlands. These areas filter rainwater and replenish underground aquifers. As the older pines in this area die and leave a space in the forest canopy, enough sunlight penetrates so that hardwoods can begin to grow to maturity.

➤At the intersection in the trail, turn to the left and walk along the bank of the Elizabeth River, where you will see the launch for the canoe trail. Across the river, a tidal wetland thrives with saltbush and big cordgrass. This marsh provides significant service, acting as a breeding ground for some organisms, a home for others, and a migratory corridor for yet others. It also provides drainage for the surrounding watershed, storage space for excess rainfall, and a filtration system for pollutants.

➤Return to and cross the main trail. At the end of the path, you will see freshwater wetlands around freshwater Turtle Lake. Look closely and you might see the lake's namesake. The hibiscus plants that grow into the lake have large pink blossoms in early summer.

➤Return to the main trail and turn right. As you walk along the riverbank, you will get another view of the lake, which was created to serve nearby farms.

➤Continue along the trail into the climax forest of oaks, maples, and hickories. Notice how different this area looks from the pine forest at the beginning of the trail. This hardwood forest produces different habitats and food sources, so you will see different kinds of birds and animals.

As you loop around the end of the trail, you will see a variety of shrubs and plants. Wild azaleas, Carolina jasmine, and holly grow abundantly. Notice the wild grapes and the fragrant white blossoms of mountain laurel. In the spring, huckleberry bushes, native to North America, grow small blue berries, a favorite of the birds and animals of the forest.

As you walk back along the riverbank, notice the large Eastern red cedar and the smaller Atlantic white cedars. The Eastern red cedar was probably planted to mark the edge of an old road. White cedars are endangered globally due to overharvesting, but they grew plentifully in the early settlement days.

➤Retrace your path through the woods to the park entrance, taking time to listen to the birdsong and smell the sweet and savory aromas of the forest.

walk 13

Red Wing Park Gardens

General location: Four miles south of the oceanfront resort beach.

Special attractions: Nature trails; Rose, Japanese, Fragrance, Conservation, and POW Memorial Gardens.

Difficulty rating: Moderate; flat, mostly paved, with 1-mile loop on dirt trail.

Distance: 2.5 miles.

Estimated time: 1.5 hours.

Services: Wheelchair-accessible restrooms; well water; horseshoes, balls, and other equipment loans.

Restrictions: Pets must be on a short leash and their droppings picked up. The park is open from 7:30 A.M. until dusk. The Nature Trail is not wheelchair accessible. The Japanese,

Red Wing Park Gardens

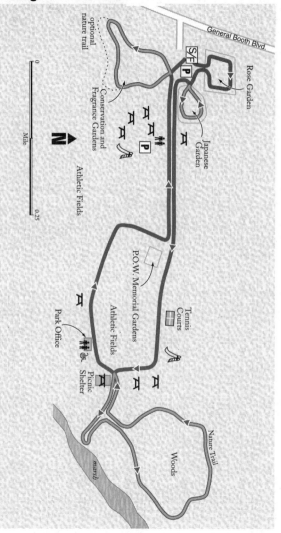

General Booth Blvd.

Rose Garden

optional
nature trail

Conservation and
Fragrance Gardens

Japanese
Garden

Athletic Fields

N

Mile

0

0.25

P.O.W.
Memorial Gardens

Athletic Fields

Tennis
Courts

Park Office

Picnic
Shelter

Nature Trail

Woods

marsh

Conservation, and Fragrance Gardens have hard-packed gravel paths, which may be difficult to negotiate in wheelchairs. Mosquitoes may be plentiful during the summer on the Nature Trail.

For more information: Contact Red Wing Park. For picnic shelter reservations, contact the Virginia Beach Parks Leisure Events office.

Getting started: This walk starts at the parking lot as you enter Red Wing Park. From the Virginia Beach oceanfront, take Pacific Avenue south. When you cross the Rudee Inlet bridge, this road becomes General Booth Boulevard. Red Wing Park is on the left, approximately 4 miles from the inlet. Park in the first parking lot on the left. If this lot is full, park in the first lot on the right.

Public transportation: Tidewater Regional Transit Route 37 departs from the oceanfront and passes Red Wing Park. Contact Tidewater Regional Transit for schedule and fare information.

Overview: On the outskirts of the oceanfront resort area, Red Wing Park consists of 90 acres of developed and undeveloped parkland. The land was acquired by the county in 1879 but was not developed as a park until 1966. The name Red Wing comes from the red-winged blackbird, which is commonly seen in the area.

In 1972, the Virginia Beach Council of Garden Clubs adopted Red Wing Park. After two years of planning, six theme gardens were created. On this walk, you will tour the Rose, Japanese, Conservation, Fragrance, and POW Memorial Gardens. These continue to thrive through the combined efforts of the garden clubs, the Parks and Recreation Department, local businesses, and private citizens' contributions.

In addition to walking in the gardens or on the nature trails, the park offers a variety of sports opportunities. If

Picnicking is one of a multitude of recreational activities that draw 570,000 visitors a year to Red Wing Park. PHOTO BY CAROLE J. ARNOLD

you did not bring equipment, you can check out basketballs, horseshoes, volleyballs, softballs and gloves, and badminton equipment by presenting a photo ID to the park attendant. Shady picnic shelters, children's playgrounds, softball diamonds, and soccer fields draw many of the 570,000 annual visitors to the park.

the walk

➤From the parking lot, walk through the arbor marking the entrance to the Rose Garden.

➤Turn left and follow the path around the perimeter of the garden. If you are walking in spring, early summer, or fall, you will enjoy the kaleidoscopic hues and delicate fragrances of more than 250 rose bushes. The garden was dedicated in 1972 to a past-president of the Council of Garden Clubs, and the council pays for its maintenance.

➤Leave the Rose Garden through the arbor. Turn left and cross the parking lot.

➤Enter the Miyazaki Japanese Garden through a shiny red gate, and bear right on the winding walkway. The gravel path may be difficult to navigate with strollers or wheelchairs.

This garden was renovated and dedicated in 1997 to mark the fifth anniversary of the sister-city relationship between Virginia Beach and Miyazaki, Japan. It contains several elements found in traditional Japanese gardens, such as a waterfall cascading over a rock wall into a small pond, a red bridge crossing a small stream, and a rock and sand garden. Adding to the exotic Far Eastern ambiance are a weeping cherry tree, heavenly bamboo, Japanese black pines, a stone pagoda, and Oriental statues. Azalea bushes, camellias, and wisteria add color when they bloom. The sense of serenity and the benches shaded by stately pines may tempt you to sit and contemplate.

►Leave through the gate and turn left to exit the parking lot.

►Turn left onto the park access road.

►Pass the POW Memorial Garden, dedicated to the many prisoners of the Vietnam War. The garden features a flagpole flying an American flag and red, white, and blue flowers in season. Three magnolia trees surround the small plaza.

►Pass the tennis courts and playground and turn right as the road curves through another parking lot. Look for the wooden picnic shelter at the far corner of the parking lot.

►Turn left off the road and walk to the left of the picnic shelter. Three signs at the edge of the woods describe the Nature Trail. Take a few minutes to study the drawings of animals, plants, and trees that you can find in the woods. Keep an eye open for raccoons, white-tailed deer, opossums, gray squirrels, pileated woodpeckers, and red-winged blackbirds. You will walk through stands of white pine, American holly, sweet gum, red maple, pin oak, loblolly pine, and sweet bay magnolia.

The Nature Trail is a dirt path obstructed by tree roots and some wet areas. It is not wheelchair or stroller accessible.

►Walk beyond the signs and follow the trail marked by white blazes painted on the trees.

►When the path splits, follow the white-blazed trail to the right into a cypress swamp. These wetlands are valuable as habitat for wildlife and as a filter for the rainwater that drains into small streams and canals and eventually enters the Atlantic Ocean. Notice the difference in the surface here. This path is covered by damp, decomposing leaves and other natural materials. It is occasionally impassable after heavy rains. On higher ground, pine needles and leaves soften the path.

➤Return to the fork in the trail and turn right. The tall evergreen trees are loblolly pines, which can reach heights of 90 feet.

➤Continue weaving through the mature forest and following the white blazes. The brown, spiny gum balls you see come from the sweet gum trees. They are a source of food for wildlife.

➤When you reach a T intersection, turn right for a short detour to the marsh.

➤Turn around and resume walking on the white-blazed trail, which winds through the woods behind the back corner of a housing development. Listen to the sounds of the woods. If you are walking in the fall, this trail blazes with the red, yellow, and orange leaves of the deciduous trees.

➤Stay on the white-blazed trail until you return to the picnic shelter.

➤Return to the paved park road and walk straight ahead, past the park office and restrooms. Sporting equipment is available at this office.

➤Follow the road as it curves back around to the park entrance. The Conservation and Fragrance Gardens will be on your left.

➤Turn left to enter the Conservation Garden and take the path to the right to circle it. This gravel path is hard-packed, but some people with strollers or wheelchairs may find it difficult to navigate in some areas.

➤As you walk, enjoy the flowers planted in this shady spot. The Conservation Garden was designed to showcase the wildflowers listed as endangered by the Virginia Federation of Garden Clubs. You also will see such annuals as marigolds and impatiens blooming in the summer.

►Enter the Fragrance Garden for the Visually Handicapped. Large gardenia bushes flanking the entranceway bloom in June. The plants in this garden were chosen for their fragrant foliage or blossoms. Signs in Braille mark the sweet pepper bushes, lilac, viburnum, gardenia, leatherleaf viburnum, red bay, wax myrtle, and other fragrant plants.

At the back of the Fragrance Garden, a nature trail leads into a wooded area. This trail, while interesting for its plant life, is not often used and can be narrow at times. This guided walk does not include the nature trail, but you may want to explore it on your own.

►Leave the Fragrance Garden and turn right to continue following the rock-lined path through the loblolly pine, maple, and oak trees.

►When you return to the entrance to the Conservation Garden, cross the park access road to the parking lot. A perfect end to this walk would be a rest on one of the benches in the fragrant Rose Garden or the peaceful Japanese Garden.

walk 14

Historic Houses on the River

General location: Explore two diverse neighborhoods and two historic houses along the Lynnhaven River just inside the mouth of Chesapeake Bay.

Special attractions: Adam Thoroughgood House, Church Point Manor House, river views.

Difficulty rating: Easy; flat, neighborhood roads, plus some sidewalks and paths.

Distance: 2 miles.

Estimated time: 1 hour.

Services: Restaurant, restrooms, gift shop.

Restrictions: Pets must be leashed and their droppings picked up.

Historic Houses on the River

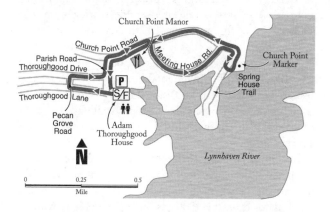

For more information: Contact the Adam Thoroughgood House or Church Point Manor House.

Getting started: From Virginia Beach/Norfolk Expressway (Route 44), take Exit 3B (Independence Boulevard). Pass the mall and the hospital. Turn right at the traffic light on Pleasure House Road. Turn right into the Thoroughgood neighborhood onto Thoroughgood Square. Turn left onto Thoroughgood Drive and then right onto Parish Road. Park in the lot of the Adam Thoroughgood House on the left.

Public transportation: Tidewater Regional Transit Route 29 passes the entrance to the Thoroughgood neighborhood. The walk begins approximately 2 miles from the entrance. Contact Tidewater Regional Transit for schedule and fare information.

Overview: Since water was the principal means of transportation in colonial Virginia, early settlers wanted to establish their homesteads along riverbanks. Adam Thoroughgood established his plantation along the western bank of the

Lynnhaven River, from which he could easily reach Chesapeake Bay and the Atlantic Ocean. The house built by one of his descendants is one of the oldest brick homes in America. It is a fine example of 17th-century architecture. Its garden is also typical of English gardens of the time.

The Thoroughgood neighborhood, which grew up around the Adam Thoroughgood House, is one of the most desirable in the city. Like Adam Thoroughgood, modern residents value their waterfront property. Today, the recreational value of the river outweighs its value as a means of transportation.

In contrast, the Church Point Manor neighborhood is a much newer development. Homes date from the 1990s and are contemporary in style. The Church Point Manor House, which dates from the 1800s, is one of the only remaining examples of the farmhouses that were built in the northern part of Virginia Beach.

You will walk on the road in Thoroughgood since there are no sidewalks, but traffic is light most of the day. There are some sidewalks in Church Point Manor. Be careful, and walk on the side of the road facing traffic when there is no sidewalk.

the walk

➤Begin this walk with a short stroll through the grounds of the Adam Thoroughgood House. Follow the brick path that leads between the gift shop and the house. Behind the house, you can explore the small English herb and flower garden and see a sliver of the Lynnhaven River; the large magnolia trees bloom in May.

➤Return to the front of the house and cross Parish Road to Thoroughgood Lane. This charming street is lined with pecan trees. As you explore the area, notice the large, mani-

of interest

The Adam Thoroughgood House

In 1621, Captain Adam Thoroughgood journeyed from England to the Virginia Colony as an indentured servant. When he returned to England a few years later, he recruited 105 settlers to follow him to Virginia. In 1635, as a reward for paying the passage of those settlers, he was given land along the Lynnhaven River. One of his descendants built this brick home around 1680. Subsequent owners remodeled the house in the early part of the 18th century as you can tell by the difference in brickwork on the east and west walls. Before Thoroughgood settled in the area, it was the site of a Chesapeake Indian village. Numerous artifacts have been found during excavations.

The house is a prime example of English cottage architecture. It was constructed with local brick and oyster-shell mortar. The leaded-glass casement windows are typical of 17th-century architecture. The house contains a spectacular collection of late 17th- and early 18th-century English furniture. The garden is also typical of 17th-century England.

cured lawns and old trees that adorn the brick ranch-style homes.

➤Turn right onto Pecan Grove Road.

➤Turn right onto Thoroughgood Drive.

➤Turn left onto Parish Road. You may think you are walking down a driveway, but it is actually part of the road. You will soon notice a small footpath at the end of the road.

➤Follow the footpath that leads between the two houses and becomes a tree-lined path. You have just entered Church

Point, one of the new neighborhoods in Virginia Beach. Notice the contrast of these large, contemporary homes with the older brick ranches of Thoroughgood.

►Turn right onto Church Point Road and walk to Church Point Manor House and the Cellars Restaurant. Church Point Manor House is one of the few remaining examples of the farmhouses that occupied the northern part of the city in the 19th century. Built in the 1860s, the house is a red-brick Victorian with Italianate detailing on the cornice, windows, and wraparound porch. The antebellum farmhouse is now a bed and breakfast inn. It has been nominated for the National Register of Historic Places.

Adam Thoroughgood once owned this land. He donated 262 acres to build a church, which was founded in 1639. The property was used to grow crops for the pastor of the church and was farmed continuously for the next 350 years.

►Turn right onto Meeting House Road and follow it around to Church Point Road.

►Turn right onto Church Point.

►Turn right onto Spring House Trail and look for a small brick marker on the bank of the Lynnhaven River. Lynnhaven Parish Church was built near this site in 1639, but the riverbank eventually eroded, destroying the church and its graveyard. The grave markers of Adam Thoroughgood and his wife, Sarah, have been recovered, as were the stones of Sarah's two later husbands.

Thoroughgood has been credited with giving the name Lynnhaven to the river and this area through which it flows. He supposedly named it after his home in King's Lynn, Norfolk County, England. In the 17th century, the word "linn" meant pool and "haven" meant an inlet of the sea or the mouth of a river. Previously called the Chesapeake River, the Lynnhaven flows into Chesapeake Bay. The area was

Built circa 1680 of local brick and oyster-shell mortar, the Adam Thoroughgood House displays a spectacular collection of antique English furniture. PHOTO COURTESY NORFOLK CONVENTION AND VISITOR BUREAU

accessible to seagoing vessels that sailed to colonial Virginia.

➤Turn around and walk on Spring House Trail back to its intersection with Church Point Road.

➤Turn left onto Church Point and walk past the Church Point Manor House.

➤Turn left at the small white sign that marks the path to the Thoroughgood House, where this walk ends.

walk 15

Back Bay

General location: Back Bay National Wildlife Refuge is on the coast at the southern end of Virginia Beach, between the Atlantic Ocean and Back Bay.

Special attractions: Wildlife habitat for threatened species such as sea turtles, peregrine falcons, and bald eagles, as well as for migrating waterfowl, including snow geese.

Difficulty rating: Easy; flat, boardwalks and hard-packed dirt trail.

Distance: 1 mile.

Estimated time: 30 minutes.

Services: Wheelchair-accessible restrooms and limited drinking water at the Visitor Contact Station, educational events and programs, electric tram from April through October.

Restrictions: Only wildlife-oriented recreation is permitted in the refuge. Swimming, sunbathing, and surfing are not allowed. Pets are allowed from October 1 through March 31 only; they must be kept on a leash. Parts of the refuge are closed at various times of year for habitat management purposes. Observe all signs marking closed areas. The refuge is open from dawn until dusk. Visitor Contact Station hours vary by season. You must pay an entry fee per vehicle.

For more information: Contact the Back Bay National Wildlife Refuge.

Getting started: This walk begins in the parking lot adjacent to the Visitor Contact Station. To reach the refuge, take General Booth Boulevard from the Virginia Beach oceanfront to Princess Anne Road. Turn left onto Princess Anne, then left again at the traffic light onto Sandbridge Road. Turn right off Sandbridge onto Sandpiper Road and follow Sandpiper through the Sandbridge community to the refuge.

Public transportation: None.

Overview: Depending on the season, Back Bay National Wildlife Refuge can be a bird watcher's paradise. Nearly 300 species of birds have been observed around the beaches, bays, and marshes of the refuge. Situated between the Atlantic Ocean and Back Bay, the refuge is an important stop along the Atlantic flyway for migrating waterfowl. Waterfowl populations have drastically declined in recent years, but the United States, Mexico, and Canada have teamed up to create the North American Waterfowl Management Plan, which is intended to help protect breeding and wintering areas. As a result, waterfowl populations are beginning to rebound. During peak migration in the fall and especially in December, approximately 10,000 snow geese and ducks visit the refuge. The sight of these large flocks of birds is spectacular.

Back Bay

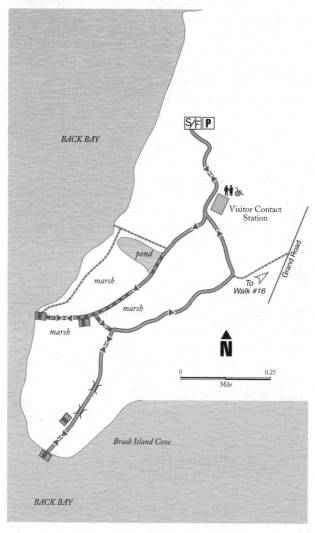

BACK BAY

S/F P

Visitor Contact
Station

pond

marsh

marsh

marsh

To
Walk #16

Grand Road

N

0   0.25
Mile

Brush Island Cove

BACK BAY

Prior to becoming a wildlife refuge in 1938, the area supported numerous hunting clubs. In the late 1800s, wealthy outdoors enthusiasts from the northeastern states flocked to these clubs to hunt the geese and ducks the refuge now protects. Now, birders from around the world visit here.

The refuge contains 7,732 acres of marsh, dunes, woodlands, and beaches. The U.S. Fish and Wildlife Service is working to acquire more land. In addition to protecting waterfowl habitat, the refuge provides habitat for other threatened and endangered species, such as loggerhead sea turtles, piping plovers, peregrine falcons, and bald eagles.

As you walk through the refuge, look for signs of wildlife, including tracks, burrows, and droppings.

the walk

➤From the parking lot, walk toward the Visitor Contact Station and take the path that passes to its right.

➤When the path forks, take the branch to the left. You will see a trail map here.

➤Pass through a small wooded area, past a pond, and continue walking straight through the marsh via the boardwalk.

➤When a section of boardwalk turns to the left, continue walking straight toward the observation deck to the right at the end of the boardwalk. From here, you will have an expansive view of Back Bay.

Approximately 105 square miles of watershed drains into Back Bay, which was saltwater until an ocean inlet south of the refuge filled up with sand in the 1830s. When the Civilian Conservation Corps built up the beach dune system in the 1930s, seawater no longer washed into the bay during storms either. The result was the emergence of the freshwater species of plants and animals you see today.

*Boardwalks that allow visitors to venture out into the wetlands
enhance wildlife viewing at Back Bay National Wildlife Refuge.*
PHOTO BY KATHERINE JACKSON

➤Return the way you came along the boardwalk. When
the boardwalk splits, turn right. Plant species here include
three-square, smartweed, spikerush, and cordgrass. You will
also pass through areas where shrubs such as wax myrtle,
high bush blueberry, bayberry, and persimmon grow abundantly. Many of these provide food for wildlife and pleasant
fragrances for passersby.

➤After crossing several wooden bridges, you will pass an observation platform on your right.

➤Cross an elevated boardwalk and continue to the end to the observation deck that overlooks the bay. If you are lucky, you may spot some of the creatures that make their home in the marsh. The white-footed mouse, which you can identify by its large eyes and ears, feeds on insects, grass, seeds, and nuts and is an important link in the food chain. Raccoons are nocturnal, but they sometimes hunt for food during the day. Their masked faces and ringed tails make them easy to identify. The muskrat is about the size of a small house cat, with a long scaly tail and glossy fur. River otters have long bodies and webbed feet. Snakes that live in the area include poisonous cottonmouths and nonpoisonous water snakes, black rat snakes, and eastern hognose snakes. Snapping turtles and other turtles often sun themselves on logs. White-tailed deer, opossums, and gray foxes also live in the marshes behind the dunes.

➤Return across the elevated boardwalk and follow the trail past the boardwalk that branches to the left. Continue along the hard-packed dirt surface.

➤At the end of the trail, you will see the Visitor Contact Station to the left. End your walk by returning to the parking lot, or explore the beaches and dikes on walk 16.

Back Bay National
Wildlife Refuge

walk 16

Beaches and Dikes

General location: Back Bay National Wildlife Refuge is on the Atlantic Coast on the southern end of Virginia Beach, between the Atlantic Ocean and Back Bay.

Special attractions: Beach walk; wildlife habitat for threatened species such as sea turtles, peregrine falcons, and bald eagles, as well as migrating waterfowl such as snow geese and tundra swans.

Difficulty rating: Difficult; flat, hard-packed dirt trail, sandy beach, and boardwalks over the dunes.

Distance: 6.5 miles.

Estimated time: 3.5 hours.

Services: Wheelchair-accessible restrooms and limited drinking water at the Visitor Contact Station, educational events and programs, electric tram from April through October.

Restrictions: Only wildlife-oriented recreation is permitted in the refuge. Swimming, sunbathing, and surfing are not allowed. Pets are not permitted. Parts of the refuge are closed at various times of the year for habitat management purposes. The portion of this walk along the dikes is closed from November through March. Observe all signs marking closed areas. The refuge is open from dawn until dusk. Visitor Contact Station hours vary by season. You must pay a vehicle entry fee.

For more information: Contact the Back Bay National Wildlife Refuge.

Getting started: This walk begins at the Visitor Contact Station.

Public transportation: None.

Overview: After walking through the marshes on the Back Bay walk, you may explore the beaches, dunes, shrub lands, and marshes that lie between the bay and the ocean. The refuge staff manages a series of impoundments in which the water level can be raised or lowered. Manipulating water levels, controlled burning, and plowing are some of the techniques used to encourage the growth of succulent marsh plants that provide food for waterfowl.

Migratory waterfowl such as swans, geese, and ducks begin entering the refuge in early fall. Approximately 10,000 snow geese winter on the refuge. Tundra swans begin to arrive in early November. Black ducks, mallards, and wood ducks nest on or near the refuge. The sight of large flocks of these birds is spectacular.

After walking along the beach, you will come to the dikes bordering the water impoundments. Depending on the time of year, you will walk on either the East Dike or the West Dike. The East Dike lies closest to the ocean and provides a

Beaches and Dikes

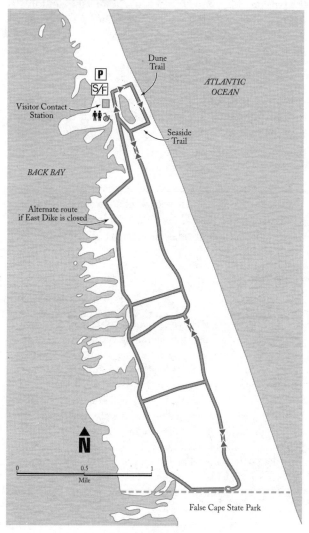

Dune Trail

ATLANTIC OCEAN

P

S/F

Visitor Contact Station

BACK BAY

Seaside Trail

Alternate route if East Dike is closed

N

0   0.5   1
Mile

False Cape State Park

better view of the dune system. The West Dike lies closer to the bay, providing a better view of the marshes and inlets. All dike trails are closed from November through March for the protection of migrating waterfowl.

the walk

➤Follow the sign to the east of the Visitor Contact Center to the seaside trail. A wooden walkway leads to the dunes.

➤Walk through the dunes until the boardwalk ends and then take the sandy path over the dune to the beach. Do not walk on the dunes except on the marked trail.

➤Turn right and walk south along the broad, flat beach. The 10- to 20-foot dunes you see change constantly due to wind, waves, and tides. These dunes protect the marsh and woodlands from high tides and storms. As you walk, look

of interest

Sea oats

The harsh coastal environment with its sandy soil, constant wind, salt spray, and scorching heat prevents all but the hardiest plants from growing. One plant that does thrive is the sea oat, which helps to stabilize and build the dunes. Its roots spread within the sand and hold the dune in place.

In the spring, sea oats look like long grass. As the weather warms, they sprout long stalks topped with green seed heads. Through the summer, these plumes dry out, turn a sandy color, and resemble common oats. Birds and rodents often eat the seeds before they have a chance to grow into new plants. In winter, sea oats turn brown and die back to the ground. The sight of sea oats blooming with fresh seed plumes in July is memorable.

for the ghost crabs that scamper along the sand and return to the ocean to wet their gills. Shorebirds include gulls, sandpipers, terns, and plovers.

The refuge beach extends nearly 3 miles to False Cape State Park. The shoreline continues through the park to the North Carolina state line, which is approximately 9 miles from the Back Bay Visitor Contact Station.

of interest

Life on the coast

It is no longer unusual to see brown pelicans soaring overhead, fishing the waters of the Atlantic Ocean. However, they were not as common in the 1950s and 1960s, when the use of DDT and other pesticides caused a decline in their population, as well as in the numbers of bald eagles and peregrine falcons. Habitat protection and bans on many pesticides have contributed to a resurgence of these birds.

In late spring or summer, loggerhead turtles mate in the shallow waters off the coast. At night, the females paddle ashore and deposit 100 to 200 eggs each in holes they dig in the sand. To increase the chances of survival for this endangered species, the refuge staff transplants the eggs to protected nurseries in the dunes, where they are less likely to be eaten by gulls, raccoons, and other predators. These reptiles can live 50 years and weigh up to 500 pounds.

The piping plover, a small, sand-colored bird, is one of the rarest shorebirds. You can identify it by its yellow-orange legs and the black ring around its neck. Some parts of the beach are closed each year to protect its nests.

Just off the coast, you may see pods of bottlenose dolphins leaping through the waves. Since they are mammals, dolphins must surface to breathe.

➤Walk approximately half a mile down the beach.

➤When you see the sign for the Dune Trail, turn right and cross the dune. Continue along the sandy path toward the elevated boardwalk. Do not cross the dunes except on the Dune Trail.

➤When you reach the gravel road, turn left to walk south on the East Dike. Notice the wooden platform that has been built to encourage nest builders.

If the East Dike is closed, turn right, walk 500 yards, and turn left onto the road along the top of the West Dike. This trail will take you closer to the bay, passing an enclosed pump station at approximately 1.5 miles. It ends at the entrance to False Cape State Park, where you will turn around and return to the parking lot. Signs clearly mark the areas that are closed.

➤Walk along the East Dike Trail, passing several cross-dikes that join the East and West Dikes. These connector trails are not open to the public.

In this area of the refuge, you may see wild hogs and horses. These are the descendants of domestic animals that escaped from nearby farms; they are not native to the refuge. They may be interesting to watch, but they compete with native species for food and cause damage to wildlife habitat.

➤When you reach the entrance to False Cape State Park, turn around and return to the parking lot along the dike to conclude your tour of the refuge. You may wish to continue walking into False Cape State Park. A visitor contact station with a restroom is approximately a mile from the entrance. There is no drinking water available in the park.

of interest

Natural events of note

Winter: Migratory waterfowl are abundant; deer shed antlers and breed.

Spring: Ospreys, egrets, and herons return from winter habitats; shorebirds nest on the beach.

Summer: Ospreys and songbirds hatch; dolphins feed and play off the coast; sea turtles nest on the beach.

Fall: Waterfowl begin to return in flocks; ospreys and martins fly south; raptors pass through on their southern migration.

walk 17

Norfolk

General location: Downtown Norfolk, its waterfront, and historic neighborhoods are 15 miles west of the Virginia Beach oceanfront.

Special attractions: Historic homes, museums, shopping malls, harbor scenes, parks, watercraft.

Difficulty rating: Moderate; flat, on paved sidewalks.

Distance: 4 miles.

Estimated time: 2 hours.

Services: Numerous restaurants, wheelchair-accessible restrooms, visitor information center.

Restrictions: Pets must be leashed and their droppings picked up. Dogs are not allowed in the Waterside Festival Marketplace.

Norfolk

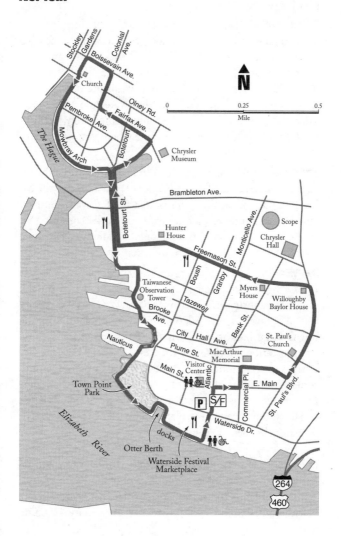

For more information: Contact the Norfolk Visitor Information Center.

Getting started: This walk begins at the City of Norfolk parking garage next to the Waterside Festival Marketplace. To get to the garage from the Virginia Beach oceanfront, take Virginia Beach/Norfolk Expressway (Route 44) west until it becomes Interstate 264. Continue westward on I-264 toward downtown Norfolk. Take the Waterside Drive exit. Turn right onto Atlantic Street and immediately left into the City of Norfolk parking garage where you will pay to park.

Public transportation: From the Virginia Beach oceanfront, Tidewater Regional Transit Route 20 goes into downtown Norfolk. Get off at St. Paul's Boulevard and walk approximately half a mile to pick up the walk at the corner of St. Paul's and Freemason Street. Contact Tidewater Regional Transit for schedule and fare information.

Overview: Norfolk history begins in 1680, when King Charles II of England decreed that cities be established on the American continent. The Towne of Lower Norfolk County was soon born. A network of rivers leading inland from the town's large harbor caused it to flourish as a seaport and transportation hub. During the Revolutionary War, the city burned to the ground as a result of British bombing and, some say, because of fires set by citizens to keep their supplies from getting into enemy hands. Only St. Paul's Episcopal Church escaped the blaze, and it remains in use today.

After decades of rebuilding, Norfolk again burned during the Civil War and was again rebuilt. Business boomed at the port of Hampton Roads, one of the largest natural harbors in the world. The establishment of the Norfolk Naval Station, which is today the largest naval installation in the world, contributed to the prosperity of the city, bringing thousands of military personnel and related businesses. One hundred ships are based in Norfolk, and more than 200,000 people live within the city's 66 square miles. Leading industries include ship repair and shipping services, rail transportation, manufacturing, medical research, the defense industry, and tourism and conventions.

Along this walk, you will see the bustling central business district, the scenic waterfront, charming historic neighborhoods, and some of the other attractions that draw visitors and area residents to the city.

the walk

➤Leave the parking garage and turn left onto Atlantic Street.

➤Walk to East Main Street. If you would like to go to the visitor information center, turn left and walk half a block. The office is across the street.

➤Otherwise, turn right onto East Main and walk 2 blocks to the statue of a Confederate soldier, a monument to those who fought for the South during the Civil War. You are walking through the central business district, where you will find banks, legal and corporate offices, and a building owned by Norfolk Southern, a Fortune 500 company.

➤Turn left onto Commercial Place. At its end you will see MacArthur Square and the four buildings of the Douglas MacArthur Memorial. General MacArthur, one of the most colorful military figures of the 20th century, is buried in the rotunda. He is perhaps best known for his role (as supreme commander) for the Allied powers after the surrender of Japan in 1945. The theater and museum feature information and memorabilia from MacArthur's life and from the

Spanish-American War, World Wars I and II, the occupation of Japan, and the Korean War. The museum complex is located in the restored 1850 city hall. The landscaped square is a pleasant place to rest.

➤Turn right onto Plume Street. At the end of Plume, you will see the current Norfolk city hall and municipal complex.

➤Turn left onto St. Paul's Boulevard. After you cross City Hall Avenue, you will pass a brick wall and a marker for the boundary of the 50 acres that comprised the original town. As you pass St. Paul's Church, look for the cannonball lodged near a stained-glass window in the brick wall.

of interest

St. Paul's Episcopal Church

Norfolk is a city of churches, and you will see many during this walk. Large trees shade St. Paul's Church, which boasts a past as unsettled as that of the city. The red brick building you see today was built in 1739. However, the history of the parish goes back much farther, as indicated by the grave markers in the cemetery, some of which date to the 1600s. The initials "SB" on the south side of the building stand for Colonel Samuel Boush, who donated the land for the church. During the Revolutionary War, the British bombarded and partially burned the church in the course of destroying the city. During the Civil War, Federal troops occupied and damaged it. As you stroll through the grounds, look for the beautiful Tiffany stained-glass window and for the cannonball in the wall, a reminder of the American Revolution.

148

➤Continue walking on St. Paul's Boulevard. You will pass one of the entrances to MacArthur Center, a mall that opened in 1999.

➤Turn left onto Freemason Street and follow the brick sidewalk. The Willoughby-Baylor House is on the corner of St. Paul's and Freemason. The Moses Myers House is at the corner of Freemason and Bank Streets.

➤Continue walking on Freemason Street. As you cross Monticello Avenue, look to the right to see the dome of the Norfolk Scope and neighboring Chrysler Hall. These

of interest

Willoughby-Baylor and Moses Myers Houses

Captain William Willoughby was a member of the merchant class that emerged after the Revolutionary War. He built the Willoughby-Baylor House in 1794 in the Georgian and Federal architectural styles that were popular at the time. The brick house and its garden and arbor reflect the domestic traditions of the 18th century. Tours are available upon request.

Just down the street is the Moses Myers House. Moses Myers holds two distinctions: he was one of America's first millionaires, and he was Norfolk's first permanent Jewish settler. His red brick house with black shutters and white columns was built during the Federal period in 1792. It is the only historic house in the nation devoted to interpreting Jewish traditions of the Revolutionary War era. It houses a collection of artwork by noted American artists such as Gilbert Stuart and Thomas Sully and furnishings that reflect the influence of the French during this period. Among Myers's notable guests were President James Monroe and Daniel Webster. This house is open to the public.

facilities offer concerts, Broadway shows, hockey matches, circuses, and other sporting and musical events.

➤Cross Granby Street, which was a center of commerce and entertainment in the early 20th century. At one time, this street was closed to automobiles, but it was later reopened to increase traffic to the shops and restaurants in the area. If you are a sports fan, you may be familiar with the name of this street. High-school wrestling teams across the country use the Granby Roll. It was developed at and named after Granby High School, a wrestling powerhouse for many years.

➤Continue on Freemason, past the stone face of Epworth Methodist Church, built in 1894.

➤Cross Boush Street. Freemason Abbey is on the corner. This former church is now a restaurant.

The red brick house on the corner of Freemason and Duke Streets, known as the Whittle House, is now the office of the Junior League. Built in 1791, it was the birthplace of Walter Taylor, a lieutenant colonel who served on Confederate General Robert E. Lee's staff during the Civil War.

➤Cross Duke Street and walk on the sidewalk beside the authentic cobblestone street. You are now touring the historic Freemason District, the oldest standing neighborhood in Norfolk. Several streets in this area are paved with cobblestones that were used as ballast in sailing ships.

The Hunter House Victorian Museum is the red building at 240 Freemason. The house was designed and built in 1894 in the Richardsonian Romanesque style. James Wilson Hunter, a prominent merchant and banker, lived in the house with his family at the turn of the 20th century. The museum includes Victorian furnishings, toys, stained-glass windows, and medical memorabilia.

Note the diverse styles of architecture you see on Freemason. While many of these beautiful buildings remain residences, others are occupied by businesses.

►Turn right onto Botetourt Street, which was named for Norborne Berkeley, Baron de Botetourt, one of the early governors of Virginia.

►Cross Brambleton Avenue and continue straight over the footbridge that crosses The Hague. Named after the homeland of one of Norfolk's prominent businessmen, The Hague anchorage basin was once a popular haven for ships voyaging up and down the Atlantic Coast. Many seamen chose to build their homes along this waterway because of its proximity to the harbor.

►Turn right onto Mowbray Arch and walk toward the Chrysler Museum.

of interest

The Chrysler Museum

Within the museum's 55 galleries, you can see a portion of a 30,000-piece art collection that spans 5,000 years. The museum is noted for its collections of Tiffany glass and photography. You will find paintings by the Renaissance masters, French Impressionists, and Abstract Expressionists. The collection also includes African, Egyptian, Pre-Columbian, and Islamic art.

The Jean Outland Chrysler Library is the largest art-reference library in the southeastern United States. The large statue of a horse and rider in front of the building is *The Torchbearers*. Artist Anna Hyatt Huntington gave it to the city in 1954. The museum theater hosts a variety of educational programs and musical performances.

➤Turn left onto Fairfax Avenue to begin a mile-long jaunt through the picturesque Ghent neighborhood. Established in 1892, Ghent was the city's first planned community. It was named after the Treaty of Ghent, which was important to the city of Norfolk because it ended the War of 1812 and reopened the embargoed port. The Page House Inn will be on your left. This Georgian Revival mansion is typical of the homes built at the turn of the 20th century, when Ghent was a fashionable place for wealthy families to settle.

➤Cross Botetourt and turn right onto Colonial Avenue.

➤Walk 2 blocks and turn left onto Boissevain Avenue. After the Civil War, a Dutchman named Adolph Boissevain financed several large projects in Norfolk, including the Norfolk and Western Railroad and the Ghent neighborhood. This street bears his name.

➤Walk 1 block and turn left onto Stockley Gardens, where you will see Christ and St. Luke's Episcopal Church. This three-story stone church, constructed in the Gothic Revival style, opened on Christmas Day 1910. Its bell tower rises 130 feet and houses a 1,218-pound bell. The nave is 55 feet high and 150 feet long and seats 800 worshippers. Stone carvings of Christ and St. Luke flank the wooden front doors on the church's exterior. The stained glass windows were made in Germany, and the ones in the clerestory were patterned after windows in the Cologne Cathedral. The church, which is listed on the National Register of Historic Places, is open to visitors.

➤Cross Olney Road and walk along The Hague on Mowbray Arch, where you will see many stately and elegant homes. After you cross Fairfax Avenue, look inside the gate at the funny fountain featuring a stone dog's head.

On the corner of Pembroke Avenue and Mowbray, look for the cream-colored brick home with the tile roof and Ionic columns; it was built around the turn of the 20th century. Again, note the diversity of architectural styles in this neighborhood, including Tudor, Federal, and Victorian. Mowbray Arch is a popular place for walking, running, and relaxing on benches under the live oak trees that line The Hague.

➤Turn right to recross the footbridge.

➤Cross Brambleton and return down Botetourt. At the corner of Botetourt and Freemason is a white wooden house, built in 1807 as the "country residence" of Dr. William B. Seldon. Confederate Army General Robert E. Lee once stayed in the house as the doctor's guest. During the Federal occupation of Norfolk from 1862 through 1865, it was seized and used by Federal commanders as a headquarters. The home is privately occupied today.

➤Walk along the brick sidewalk that fronts the harbor and small marina.

➤At the intersection of Botetourt and College Place, continue walking straight into College Place and follow the brick pavement around to the right, past the buildings and to the waterfront.

➤Turn left and then immediately right on the brick sidewalk and walk toward the Taiwanese Observation Tower. This ornate building commemorates a 1983 visit to this site by Dr. Lee Teng-Hui, who was president of the Republic of China and then governor of Taiwan Province.

Take a moment to look across the harbor; you can see the Portsmouth waterfront and the red brick buildings of the Portsmouth Naval Hospital. Colonel William Crawford established the town of Portsmouth in 1752.

As you walk along the waterfront, you will likely see all sorts of pleasure craft, sailboats, barges, tugboats, military ships, and touring boats. Hampton Roads is among the leading ports in the United States; it handles more waterborne foreign commerce than any other U.S. port. The waterfront can be bustling or serene, depending on the time of day and the weather.

➤Follow the brick sidewalk between the ornamental tower and the river.

➤Cross Brooke Avenue. The gray building you see in front of you is Nauticus, the National Maritime Center.

➤Follow the brick sidewalk until you come to a boardwalk that crosses a section of the river. At the end of the board-walk, take the brick sidewalk that leads around the front of Nauticus and back to the waterfront.

➤Continue walking along the waterfront through Town Point Park, which was built in 1983. Before redevelopment and the construction of this 7-acre park and the adjacent

of interest

Nauticus, the National Maritime Center

This educational facility is part interactive museum, part science center, and part aquarium. Its hands-on exhibits include stations at which visitors can "land" a jet fighter on an aircraft carrier or fight a mock naval battle. They can pet a shark, forecast the weather, and, in a virtual-reality game, search for the eggs of the Loch Ness monster. A large-screen theater features the movie *The Living Sea*, which was nominated for an Academy Award. The Hampton Roads Naval Museum, one of ten museums operated by the U.S. Navy, is located within Nauticus. Exhibits highlight naval battles that have occurred in the Norfolk area, including the Battle Off the Capes during the Revolutionary War and the clash of the *Monitor* and the *Virginia*, also known as the *Merrimac*, during the Civil War.

The construction of Waterside Festival Marketplace, a complex of shops and restaurants on the Norfolk waterfront, was a catalyst for renovation of the city core. PHOTO COURTESY OF NORFOLK CONVENTION AND VISITORS BUREAU

Waterside Festival Marketplace, this harbor area was an eyesore. Today the park hosts more than 100 free events each year, including the Bayou Boogaloo & Cajun Food Festival, the Town Point Jazz & Blues Festival, the Virginia Children's Festival, Harborfest, and various concerts and events.

Tall sailing ships from around the world visit the harbor and dock at Waterside to participate in festivals and host tours. The Waterside Festival Marketplace houses 75 restaurants and shops selling everything from seafood to Virginia products to T-shirts.

Between the park and the marketplace is Otter Berth, home of the *Spirit of Norfolk*. This ship, along with the *American Rover* and *Carrie B*, provide tours of the harbor.

►Walk around Otter Berth and turn right; then turn left to return to the waterfront. The marina you pass provides a port for a variety of working and pleasure crafts, as well as a temporary haven for boat travelers. The Elizabeth River ferry and water taxis, which transport passengers between Norfolk and Portsmouth, dock in this area. The Tugboat Museum aboard the 1933 tugboat *Huntington* tells the story of these "workhorses of the waterways," which help aircraft carriers, submarines, passenger ships, and barges dock in the busy harbor. You can tour the wheelhouse, crew's quarters, and engine room of the *Huntington*.

►When you reach Waterside Festival Marketplace, walk through the building and cross Waterside Drive to return to the parking garage and end your adventure in Norfolk.

walk 18

Hampton

General location: Located 30 miles from the Virginia Beach oceanfront, this walk explores downtown Hampton and its waterfront.

Special attractions: Aerospace museum, antique carousel, marinas, historic sites, boutiques, numerous restaurants.

Difficulty rating: Easy; flat, entirely on sidewalks.

Distance: 2.5 miles.

Estimated time: 1.5 hours.

Services: Visitor information center and museum with wheelchair-accessible restrooms, restaurants, shops.

Restrictions: Pets must be leashed and their droppings picked up.

For more information: Contact the Hampton Visitor Center.

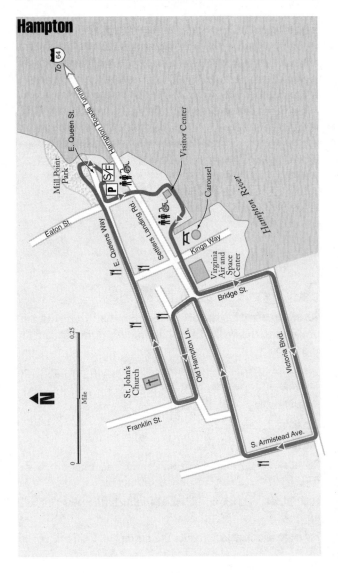

Hampton

Getting started: This walk begins at the parking garage at the corner of Settlers Landing Road and Eaton Street in Hampton. From the Virginia Beach oceanfront, take Virginia Beach/Norfolk Expressway (Route 44) west to Interstate 64 west. Go north on I-64 through the Hampton Roads Bridge-Tunnel and take Exit 267 to downtown Hampton. Turn left at the end of the ramp. Turn right onto Settlers Landing Road. At the foot of the bridge, turn right onto Eaton Street. Take the first right onto East Queen Street and enter the parking garage, where you will pay to park.

Public transportation: Tidewater Regional Transit Route 61 departs from Pembroke East in Virginia Beach and runs to the Hampton Transportation Center on Pembroke Avenue daily except Sundays. From the center, walk 2 blocks east to Eaton Street, turn right, and walk 3 blocks on Eaton to the parking garage to begin the walk. Call Tidewater Regional Transit for schedule and fare information.

Overview: English presence in Hampton, originally called Kecoughtan, dates back to 1607, when Captain John Smith and the *Susan Constant, Discovery,* and *Godspeed* stopped there briefly on their way up the James River to settle Jamestown. The following year, English colonists visited the Kecoughtan Indians in Hampton to share oysters and fish at the first Christmas dinner in the New World. One year later, a wooden fort was built to protect the new colony from Spanish raiders. Because of its location on Hampton Roads Harbor and the James River, the growing fishing village became a popular stopping place as the young nation developed. Hampton burned to the ground during the Civil War, but since that time it has grown into a city of 55 square miles with a population of approximately 138,000.

Surrounded as it is by Hampton Roads Harbor, the James River, and Chesapeake Bay, Hampton relies primarily on

shipbuilding, shipping and rail transportation, seafood pro-
duction, the military, and tourism as its major industries.
Public and private marinas line the shores. The city's location on the Atlantic Intracoastal Waterway—a continuous
system of sheltered inland channels—makes it a popular stop
for recreational boaters along the East Coast.

In addition to the first Christmas celebration, Hampton
claims many other firsts: It is the oldest English-speaking
U.S. settlement still in existence, the first town in the United
States to offer free public education, the first city to provide
organized education to African-Americans, and the first
training ground for U.S. astronauts.

This walk will introduce you to the downtown Hampton waterfront and the surrounding neighborhood with its
colorful marinas, historic brick buildings, Victorian houses,
and pedestrian-friendly streets. There are several other places
you may want to explore. They include Fort Monroe, the
largest stone fort ever built in the United States. The Casemate Museum, located inside the fort, exhibits the cell in
which Confederate President Jefferson Davis was impris-
oned after the Civil War, as well as Civil War memorabilia.
Fort Wool, which protected the entrance to Hampton Roads
Harbor during the Civil War, is accessible by tour boat.
Hampton University, founded in 1868 as an institute of
higher learning for newly freed slaves, boasts six historic
landmarks on campus.

the walk

➤Leave the parking garage the way you came in and turn
left onto East Queen Street.

➤Turn left onto Eaton Street and walk across Settlers Landing Road.

➤Walk through the brick parking lot and the tree-lined plaza to the Hampton Visitor Center. You are walking along the Hampton River. Tour boats depart from this site to explore Hampton from the water, offering views of Hampton Roads, Fort Monroe, and Fort Wool.

➤Walk along the dock behind the visitor center. You will see part of the armada of pleasure boats that dock in Hampton. Across the water, you can see part of the Hampton University campus and some of the commercial boats that ply the local waters for seafood.

➤After you circle the visitor center, continue walking along the waterfront.

of interest

Hampton Carousel

Take a ride back into childhood on the Hampton Carousel. This merry-go-round began operating in 1921 at the Buckroe Beach Amusement Park in Hampton. Its horses and chariots were carved from hardwood and painted by German, Italian, and Russian immigrant artisans who worked for the Philadelphia Toboggan Company. The carousel operated at the amusement park until the park closed in 1985. Unwilling to lose this colorful piece of American folk art, Hampton residents and businesses joined the city in raising funds to restore the carousel. After two years of painstaking stripping, repairing, and painting, the carousel was installed in this pavilion. It still has all of its original mirrors and oil paintings. The 48 horses rise and fall to the music of the original organ. The carousel is one of fewer than 200 antique carousels still operating in the United States. Even if you are not interested in riding, the intricately carved and painted horses are worth a look.

➤At the end of the dock, turn right and then left toward the Virginia Air and Space Center, which you can see in front of you.

➤Walk through the plaza, where you will see the Hampton Carousel.

➤Cross Kings Way and walk along Settlers Landing.

➤Turn left onto Bridge Street and walk past a commercial seafood processing plant, one of the family seafood

of interest

Virginia Air and Space Center

If you are interested in flight, you will love this museum. Nineteen aircraft and spacecraft hang from the ceiling of this visitor center for the NASA Langley Research Center. They include an F-4E "Phantom" fighter used during the Vietnam War and a "Delta Dart" that was struck nearly 700 times by lightning while flying through storms as part of NASA lightning research. Other exhibits include the Apollo 12 command module that traveled to the moon and back and the Langley Aerodrome, whose inventor was competing with the Wright Brothers to achieve the first manned flight.

In addition to aircraft displays, the center offers hands-on exhibits where visitors can "be" an astronaut, "launch" a rocket, and ride in a motion simulator. A five-story IMAX movie theater features aeronautical and adventure movies. The Hampton Roads History Center, housed in the same building, looks into the history of the area, from the days of the Kecoughtan Indians to the colonial era to the Civil War. The Battle of the Ironclads between the USS *Monitor* and the CSS *Virginia* (also known as the *Merrimac*) is also depicted. Tours of the NASA Langley research facility depart from the center.

The roofline of the Virginia Air and Space Center, Hampton, is reminiscent of the wings of a bird in flight. PHOTO COURTESY OF HAMPTON CONVENTIONS AND TOURISM

businesses that has operated for generations on the Hampton waterfront. On this portion of the walk, you will pass water-related businesses such as sail makers and equipment purveyors that support the recreational and commercial boats in the area.

➤Walk 3 blocks past the marina to Victoria Boulevard. At the corner of Bridge and Victoria, a cannon commemorates the 1755 arrival near this site of Edward Braddock, major general and commander-in-chief of all the British forces in America before the Revolution.

➤Turn right onto Victoria and enjoy walking several blocks along this shady street with its charming Victorian homes. Modest clapboard homes with wraparound porches sit among brick mansions with turret towers and arched windows.

➤Turn right onto South Armistead Avenue. On your left, you will see Magnolia House. The architecture of this 19th-

of interest

St. John's Episcopal Church

Established in 1610, St. John's Parish is the oldest continuous English-speaking parish in the United States. The church you see was built in 1728, but its cemetery contains gravestones that date back as far as 1701. Designed in the shape of a Latin cross, the small brick church has walls that are 2 feet thick. Nonetheless, it was damaged during the Revolutionary War and the War of 1812 and was neglected for years.

After a restoration in 1825, the church was charred by fires set by Hampton residents to keep the town out of Federal control during the Civil War. Union soldiers camped in the churchyard, beside the blackened walls. The church was restored again after the war, and additional improvements have been made since. It is now a Virginia Historic Landmark and is listed on the National Register of Historic Places.

The church's Pocahontas window was donated in 1887, in part by Indian students who attended the forerunner of Hampton University. The Colonial Clergy window lists the names of colonial-era rectors. When the window was installed in 1903, the acting rector objected to listing one of his predecessors, Jeremiah Taylor, because Taylor reportedly liked "things of the flesh." The compromise was to bracket his name on the window as a lasting reminder of his bad reputation. The prized possession of the church is a silver communion service made in London in 1618.

In the cemetery, look for the memorial to church member Virginia Laydon, who was born in 1609 and was the first surviving child born in the New World to English parents. Virginia's father arrived in the New World aboard the *Susan Constant*. The Hannah Nicholson Tunnel memorial in the cemetery commemorates a woman who crossed Union lines to warn the Confederate Army of an impending advance.

century home, now a restaurant and antique shop, is described as Free Classic Queen Anne with gingerbread motif. A prominent Hampton citizen who served as a harbor pilot and made his fortune by bringing moving pictures to Hampton built the house around 1855. The number of columns decorating the downstairs was once an indication of the wealth and position of the owners. The magnolia trees and iron fence surrounding the house also harken back to the Victorian era.

►Turn right on Settlers Landing and pass several antique shops and galleries in restored Victorian homes.

►Turn left onto Bridge Street.

►Turn left onto Old Hampton Lane and walk along Queens Way Mall, where you will find a variety of boutiques. The Grey Goose Tea Room is a local favorite.

►Turn right onto Franklin Street.

►Turn right onto East Queens Way. On the left is St. John's Episcopal Church and cemetery with its wrought-iron fence and tall monument "to our Confederate dead." An entrance ramp for those with strollers and wheelchairs is located at the back of the church.

►Walk several blocks on East Queens Way. Along this popular restaurant row you will find everything from Southern cooking to nouvelle cuisine to sushi. Several historic buildings on this street have been renovated and are marked with plaques. On the left side of the street, the Sclater Building, the oldest surviving commercial structure in Old Hampton, was built just after the Civil War. It now houses the law firm of one of the original owner's descendants.

►Cross Eaton Street to walk through Mill Point Park. This popular gathering point hosts musical and theatrical performances in its small waterfront amphitheater.

➤Take the path that leads to the river and behind the stage. The parking garage where this walk begins and ends is now in front of you.

of interest

Other highlights from Hampton history

1570: Spanish explorers arrive at Kecoughtan (later named Hampton).

1634: Benjamin Syms bequeaths his property for the establishment of the first free school in the country.

1829: Edgar Allan Poe is promoted to sergeant major at Fort Monroe.

1918: Author Thomas Wolfe works as a laborer at Langley Field, then administered by the National Advisory Committee for Aeronautics, and later draws on his experiences there to write the novel *Look Homeward, Angel*.

1959: The first astronauts in the country, including John Glenn and Alan B. Shepard Jr., are trained at NASA Langley Research Center.

1972: The National Municipal League chooses Hampton as an "All-American City."

walk 19

Colonial Williamsburg

General location: This walk explores the streets of the restored colonial town of Williamsburg, which is approximately 60 miles from the Virginia Beach oceanfront. The scenic Colonial Parkway joins Colonial Williamsburg and Jamestown (walk 20).

Special attractions: The restored streets and buildings of a colonial American town, costumed historical interpreters, College of William and Mary, modern and period shops and taverns.

Difficulty rating: Easy; flat, mostly on paved sidewalks.

Distance: 2.5 miles.

Estimated time: 1.5 hours.

Services: Wheelchair-accessible restrooms in the visitor center, restaurants, refreshment stands.

Colonial Williamsburg

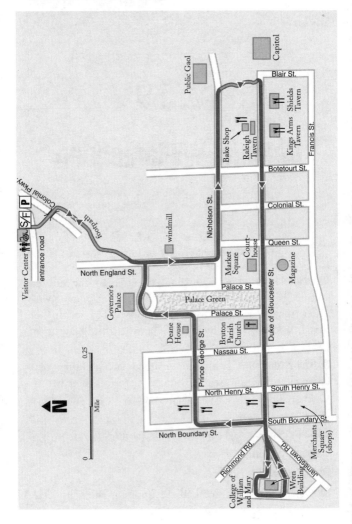

Restrictions: During the day, the streets of the restored area are closed to vehicles other than those belonging to residents, but they are open to pedestrians. Many buildings and fenced or walled areas of the village are only open to those who purchase a visitor pass at the visitor center. Each day, various exhibit buildings are open, with costumed historical interpreters engaged in colonial activities. A visitor pass is necessary for most of these buildings. The *Visitor's Companion*, available at the visitor center, includes a schedule of plays and reenactments. Some shops and taverns in the colonial area do not require a visitor pass; however, reservations are recommended for dining in the historic taverns. Seeing and hearing the historic reenactments will add to your learning experience in Colonial Williamsburg, but the restored town also provides a pleasant setting for those who simply wish to stroll the streets and wander through the open gardens. Special accommodations for people with disabilities can be arranged at the visitor center.

For more information: Contact the Colonial Williamsburg Foundation.

Getting started: This walk begins at the Colonial Williamsburg Visitor Center. From the Virginia Beach oceanfront, take Virginia Beach/Norfolk Expressway (Route 44) west to Interstate 64 west. Head north on I-64 and cross the Hampton Roads Bridge-Tunnel. When you reach the Williamsburg area, follow the signs for Colonial Williamsburg by taking Exit 238, Virginia Route 143 east. Turn left onto Virginia Route 132 south and left again onto VA 132Y. Park in the free lot at the visitor center and spend a few minutes exploring the center. Two free films provide an overview of the colonial capital and its history.

Public transportation: None.

Overview: The renovated and restored buildings and streets of Colonial Williamsburg recreate the 18th-century capital of the British colony of Virginia, which later became the capital of the American Commonwealth of Virginia. Williamsburg was established as the center of government in the colony in 1699, after the statehouse in the 17th-century capital, Jamestown, burned for the fourth time. Formerly known as Middle Plantation, this growing village was chosen because of its location on high ground between the James and York Rivers, its proximity to Jamestown (5 miles away), and its growing popularity with prosperous tobacco planters and merchants. In addition, the College of William and Mary had been established here in 1695, and many leading politicians lived nearby.

After deciding to move the capital, civic leaders adopted a town plan with a large open square and a wide "main street" leading from the Capitol "downtown" to the College of William and Mary "uptown." The Governor's Palace became the focal point of a broad parkland avenue adjacent to the main street. The prominent locations of Bruton Parish Church, the college, the Governor's Palace, and the Capitol underscore the importance of religion, education, and government in colonial America.

This walk leads you through the streets of the colonial capital. You will see where early Americans lived, shopped, worshipped, and enacted laws to govern the English colony and later the American state.

the walk

➤Leave the visitor center by the door that leads to the parking lot designated "blue."

➤Turn right onto the sidewalk and cross the entrance road.

Costumed interpreters parade through the renovated streets of Colonial Williamsburg, the 18th-century capital of the British colony of Virginia. PHOTO COURTESY OF THE COLONIAL WILLIAMSBURG FOUNDATION

►Turn left to walk along the gravel footpath that leads to the historic area, going under a red brick bridge and beside a small stream. The road beside the footpath is Colonial Parkway, a scenic route that connects Jamestown, Williamsburg, and Yorktown.

►Turn left onto North England Street at the end of the footpath and walk past the windmill. You are passing the rural-trades area, where artisans make bricks, shingles, barrels, and other necessities. These fields are planted with some of the crops that were important to the colony, such as corn, tobacco, and wheat.

(*Author's note: Remember, many of the buildings and gardens you pass are open only to visitors who purchase a pass at the visitor center. Costumed interpreters staff the entrances to exhibit areas. If you see an open gate or door without an interpreter, you are most likely free to wander in without a pass. Please heed all "Private Entrance Only" signs.*)

►Turn left onto Nicholson Street. You are walking through what was a residential area in colonial days. Houses, shops, work sheds, kitchens, smokehouses, stables, livestock pens, and privies would have lined streets like this in the 18th century. On the right side of the road, notice the brown-brick building with the white fence and the pigeon coop on its roof.

►Cross Botetourt Street and walk toward the jail.

►Turn right onto the footpath that crosses a small wooden bridge and walk beside the Secretary's House. At the end of the footpath, the Capitol will be on your left.

►Turn right onto Duke of Gloucester Street. This was the center of commerce in colonial days. Merchants lived and worked in the taverns and shops, serving those who lived in town or came to conduct business in the capital. Shields

of interest

The Capitol

The structure you see today was reconstructed on the foundations of the original building. The House of Burgesses and the Council were the two houses of the legislature in Virginia in the 18th century. They met in the Capitol and ruled England's largest and most populous colony for 80 years. Patrick Henry gave his famous "Caesar-Brutus" speech here. The resolution declaring Virginia's independence from Britain was adopted here on May 15, 1776. Thomas Jefferson wrote his bill calling for religious freedom in this building. In addition to legislative meetings, the Capitol was the site of the General Court, the highest court in the colony, which met twice each year.

Tavern and Kings Arms Tavern on the left side of the road serve traditional meals and do not require visitor passes. Servers wear 18th-century costumes, and strolling musicians sing the same ballads that Thomas Jefferson and George Wythe heard when they stopped in for a hearty meal. "Publick" houses such as these played a key role in colonial life as a place for food, drink, and accommodations for travelers.

On the right side of the road is Raleigh Tavern where, in 1796, members of the House of Burgesses adopted a proposal to boycott British goods. Five years later they met here and issued a call for delegates from all the colonies to meet at the Continental Congress.

Behind Raleigh Tavern, you will find a bakeshop that is open to the public. Costumed characters sell gingerbread cookies, Sally Lund bread, cider, and lemonade. Two shops that do not require passes are the jewelry store and Tarpley & Company, where you can purchase hats and reproductions of

18th-century merchandise. The millinery shop and the wig maker do require visitor passes.

➤Cross Botetourt Street and continue walking through the commercial area. The grocery shop on the right sells wine, Virginia hams, and other products from the period. The Post Office is open to the public without a pass; along with the Printing Office, it served as the town's communications center, selling books and newspapers, providing mail service, and producing public documents.

➤Cross Queen Street and enter Market Square.

➤Walk past Palace Green. This sweeping lawn with its lush grass and decorative catalpa trees provides a grand view of the Governor's Palace.

➤Pass Bruton Parish Church, which you can tour without a visitor pass. Before Williamsburg became the colonial capital, this church was the most important public building in Middle Plantation. Used continuously since 1715, it is one of the oldest Episcopal churches in the nation. Both whites and slaves worshipped here, although they sat apart. Students from the College of William and Mary also attended services. Their carved initials can still be seen in the wooden handrail. A walk through the cemetery with its magnolia, cedar, and sycamore trees reveals the graves of some of the colony's most prominent citizens, including a royal governor, Francis Fauquier.

➤Cross Nassau and Henry Streets to enter the modern Merchants Square. Here you will find shops selling both modern and reproduction merchandise such as pewter, toys, Virginia products, books, and clothing. The Trellis Restaurant is one of the most renowned and upscale restaurants in Williamsburg.

➤At the end of Merchants Square, cross Boundary Street and pass through the gates to the campus of the College of

Market Square

This was the center of town and a center of public life. It was the site of daily markets and annual fairs. In the morning before dawn, the square would come alive with people selling farm produce, meat, pottery, clothing, baskets, and toys. Since they had no refrigeration, citizens purchased fresh provisions each day. By mid-morning, the market would begin to disassemble and the taverns nearby would come to life with farmers and shoppers seeking gossip and something with which to quench their thirst. Colonial fairs twice a year brought games, music, dancing, puppet shows, and horse races to the square. Auctions of slaves, goods, and land occurred here.

The Courthouse, built on the square in 1770 and used until 1932, provided space for the government and courts of Williamsburg and James City County. Magistrates met here to levy taxes, mediate property disputes, and regulate affairs of the town and county. The County Court tried people accused of small crimes, whereas the General Court, which met in the Capitol, tried accused felons. Convicts were often punished immediately at the whipping post and stockade in the square. The square also functioned as a training field for the local militia, which was comprised of every free, white, healthy, male British subject between the ages of 16 and 60. Public notices, celebrations, and elections also occurred on the square.

The Magazine, the octagonal-shaped brick building on the south side of the street, served as the arsenal for firearms, gunpowder, and military equipment. The building you see was constructed in 1715.

of interest

College of William and Mary

King William and Queen Mary of England chartered the College of William and Mary in 1693. The sons of prestigious Virginia families attended the school, which was the center of higher education in the colony. Only about 100 students attended classes during the 18th century, but the institution had a strong influence on political and intellectual life of the time. Construction of the Wren Building began in 1695. Three separate fires have damaged it over the years, but the exterior brick has remained unharmed. The walls you see are mostly original.

The General Assembly met in this building from 1700 to 1704 while the Capitol was being constructed, and again from 1747 to 1754 while fire damage to the Capitol was being repaired. The Wren Building is the oldest academic building in continuous use in the United States. To your left is the Brafferton Building, constructed in 1723 as a school for Indians. To your right is the President's House, built in 1732. French soldiers accidentally burned the building in 1781, but the French king Louis XVI repaired the damage five years later.

William and Mary. The Wren Building, at the center of the lawn, does not require a visitor pass.

➤Walk down the sidewalk in the center of the lawn, past the statue of Norborne Berkeley, Baron de Botetourt and governor of the Colony of Virginia from 1768 to 1770.

➤Turn right and walk around the Wren Building for a brief tour of the campus. The buildings you see are still used today for academic purposes.

➤Turn left behind the Wren Building and walk along the shady sidewalk.

➤Turn left and walk past the building to return to the gate on Boundary Street.

➤Turn left onto North Boundary.

➤Turn right onto Prince George Street. Pubs and clubs that serve the college students are located in this area. You might want to stop at the Cheese Shop on Prince George for a sandwich and then find a place to eat it on nearby Palace Green.

➤Cross North Henry Street. When you cross Nassau Street, you will reenter the historic area. As you approach the Deane House on your left, you will notice a small white pigeon coop on stilts to your right. At the apex of the roof of the white house nearby, notice the bar that was used to lift furniture and supplies to the second story with a rope and pulley.

The grounds of the Deane House are open to the public. This white wooden home with black shutters and white picket fence was typical of the homes of the Virginia gentry. Elkanah Deane was an Irish coach maker who prospered in the colony. Notice the well, cellar doors, linden trees, topiary, and outbuildings. Wheelwrights, blacksmiths, and harness makers built carriages in the shop behind the house.

➤Turn left onto Palace Street. The upper-crust gentry owned residences here, as it was close to the Governor's Palace.

➤Pass the McKenzie Apothecary, which does not require a visitor pass. Dr. McKenzie lived and worked on this property and sold some of the same items available today.

➤Turn right in front of the Governor's Palace.

of interest

Governor's Palace

This three-story brick building reigned supreme over Palace Green and the surrounding one-story homes of the gentry. The golden crowns on the gate and on the cupola symbolize the governor's connection to royalty. Seven royal governors who represented the King of England in the British colony and the first two governors of the Commonwealth of Virginia lived and entertained lavishly in this imposing residence.

The palace features a grand entrance hall, a ballroom, and a wide staircase leading to a "middle room" where the governor received official guests. The palace grounds contain a stable, kitchen, and gardens. During the American Revolution, the royal governor fled the palace, and it was used as a hospital during the siege of Yorktown.

➤Turn left onto North England Street.

➤Turn right onto the footpath, which will take you out of the 18th-century colonial capital and back to the 20th-century visitor center.

walk 20

Jamestown

General location: Colonial National Historical Park /Jamestown is located between the James and York Rivers, approximately 60 miles from Virginia Beach. The Colonial Parkway joins Jamestown and Colonial Williamsburg (walk 19).

Special attractions: Historic church and town site, visitor center, interpretive signs on walking path, James River views.

Difficulty rating: Easy; dirt paths.

Distance: 1.25 miles.

Estimated time: 1.5 hours.

Services: Wheelchair-accessible restrooms, water fountains, educational movie, rental tapes, and exhibits at visitor center.

Restrictions: Pets must be leashed at all times and their droppings picked up. The park is open from 9 A.M. until dusk. The visitor center closes earlier.

Jamestown

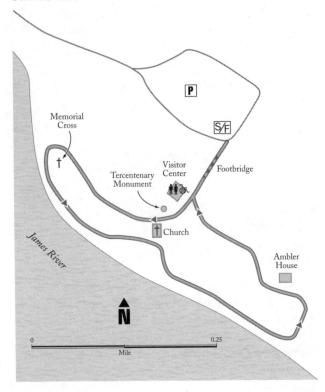

P

S/F

Memorial
Cross

Tercentenary
Monument

Visitor
Center

Footbridge

Church

James River

Ambler
House

N

0   0.25
Mile

For more information: Contact Colonial National Historical Park/Jamestown or the Association for the Preservation of Virginia Antiquities.

Getting started: This walk begins in the parking lot of Colonial National Historical Park/Jamestown. From the Virginia Beach oceanfront, take Virginia Beach/Norfolk Expressway (Route 44) west to Interstate 64. Take I-64 north and cross the Hampton Roads Bridge-Tunnel. Take Jamestown Exit 242A and follow Virginia Route 199 west to Virginia Route 31. Turn left and you will soon come to the entrance station for the park. Follow the road approximately a mile to the parking lot.

Public transportation: None.

Overview: After English sailors aboard the *Godspeed, Susan Constant*, and *Discovery* landed at the mouth of Chesapeake Bay in 1607, they traveled up the James River looking for a place to establish a settlement. These 104 men and boys, including Captain John Smith, had been sent by the Virginia Company, which was chartered by King James I to explore the New World and establish an English foothold in America. The small ships, one of them only about the size of a school bus, arrived at Jamestown Island in May, and Jamestown became and remains the first permanent English settlement in the New World.

The colonists chose to stop here, about 60 miles up the river, because the deepest part of the river flowed close to land, making it easy to moor their ships. Although Algonquin Indians immediately attacked, the newcomers dug in and constructed a wooden fort for protection. Within six months of their arrival, 50 settlers had died of disease and starvation. Lack of an adequate water supply also made life difficult.

Two years later, with the arrival of new settlers, the population of the settlement had grown to about 500. However, all but 60 of them died during the winter of 1609–1610 in what was known as "the Starving Time." With continued support from England and the arrival of supply ships, the colony eventually recovered. Relations with the Algonquins improved with the marriage of Pocahontas, daughter of Indian Chief Powhatan, to English colonist John Rolfe in 1614.

The first representative legislative assembly in North America met in Jamestown 12 years after the town was founded. Jamestown remained the colonial capital until 1698, when a fire burned the statehouse. The capital was moved to Williamsburg that year. Eventually, the Jamestown settlement dwindled, and the area was used as farmland.

The National Park Service, U.S. Department of the Interior, and Association for the Preservation of Virginia Antiquities jointly manage the original settlement site. Nearby, the Jamestown-Yorktown Foundation operates the Jamestown Settlement, a recreation complete with costumed interpreters and replicas of the fort and the three English ships. The 23-mile-long Colonial Parkway connects Jamestown to Williamsburg and to Yorktown, where one of the decisive battles of the American Revolution was fought.

In addition to taking this walk through the fort and the New Towne and along the James River, you may want to walk or drive the 3- and 5-mile self-guided loops. These tours of the island have interpretive signs to enhance your understanding of Jamestown and its role in the birth of the nation, and they provide a view of the natural environment that greeted the settlers.

the walk

➤Begin this walk at the parking lot of the Jamestown Island Visitor Center. Follow the sidewalk from the parking lot to a wooden footbridge, and follow the path to the front of the building. The center shows a 15-minute movie that explains Jamestown history. Exhibits include artifacts, ship models, and dioramas depicting the fort, the frontier lifestyle, and subsequent development.

As you walk, consider how it felt to land on this uninhabited island. Could you have endured the icy winters and blazing summers with only wooden structures for shelter? Could you have survived the terror of Indian attacks and the sadness of losing your compatriots to disease and starvation? If you can imagine the commitment to succeed in spite of these obstacles, you will understand the foundation on which this settlement and the young country was built.

➤Walk past the visitor center toward the Tercentenary Monument. This granite shaft is 103 feet tall and was constructed in 1907 to commemorate the 300th anniversary of the arrival of the settlers from England.

➤Take the dirt path that turns to the right, and pass through the iron gate in the brick wall. The church tower on the left is the only remaining 17th-century structure on the site. It was a 1647 addition to the original church that was built in 1617. The original frame structure was the first Anglican church in Virginia and the place where the first representative legislative assembly in North America met on July 30, 1619. In 1907, a brick church was built as a memorial on the original foundation.

➤Walk to the end of the path, where you will see the Memorial Cross, which marks the graves of hundreds of settlers who died during the bleak winter of 1609–1610, known as "the Starving Time."

You will also see where the third and fourth statehouses once stood. The bricks you see are not the original foundations. Those lie under the bricks, which protect the original structures and mark the sites for visitors. When the fourth statehouse burned in 1698, the general assembly moved the capital to Williamsburg.

➤Follow the path along the James River, which served as a major highway in the 17th century. Ships sailing upriver brought seeds, food, and tools to the settlers and took tobacco, timber, and furs back to England. You are walking on a seawall built by the U.S. Army Corps of Engineers in the early 1900s to protect the historical site from erosion. The James River leads all the way to the current capital of the Commonwealth of Virginia in Richmond.

➤Walk through the church gate and to the right of the church. Close to the river, you can see an ongoing archeological project. This dig has uncovered evidence that the original James Fort was located inland from the current shoreline. Experts had believed that the fort site was now underwater.

As you continue along the river, you will enter the area known as New Towne. This is where the settlement expanded as new colonists arrived. Brick houses replaced wooden structures as residents prospered, mainly from the tobacco trade. Some accounts report that tobacco was even grown in the streets of the town.

➤Follow the trail until it curves to the left. You will pass the remains of Ambler House, which was built in the 1750s.

➤Follow the path as it angles to the right.

➤Return to the visitor center and cross the footbridge to the parking lot to complete your walk through the first permanent English settlement in the New World.

Appendix A: Other Sights

Some other sights in the area may or may not require much walking, but they are popular with tourists and residents. If you have the time, they are worth a visit.

In Virginia Beach

Lynnhaven House, 4401 Wishart Road, 757-460-1688.

This brick house is on the bank of the Lynnhaven River. It is a fine example of 18th-century eastern Virginia vernacular architecture. Programs feature the skills, crafts, and games that were popular in the Virginia colony when the house was built in 1725.

Francis Land House, 3431 Virginia Beach Boulevard, 757-431-4000.

This gracious plantation house is alive with the sounds, smells, and sights of the 18th-century. Costumed interpreters provide programs on topics such as flax and linen, children's games, barrel making, and candle making. The gardens and exhibits reveal what life was like in Virginia Beach more than 200 years ago.

Oceana Naval Air Station, Oceana Boulevard, 757-433-3131.

Oceana is one of the largest master jet bases in the world and home to the Navy's F-14 Tomcat and the F/A-18 Hornet fighter jets. Tours are available via Tidewater Regional Transit trolleys, departing from 24th Street Park. You can also tour the Aviation Historical Park on your own. The park is just inside the main gate on Oceana Boulevard. To watch jets in flight, visit one of the observation parks on London Bridge Road and Oceana Boulevard.

In Norfolk

Norfolk Botanical Garden, 6700 Azalea Garden Road, 757-441-5830.

Depending on the season, thousands of roses, azaleas, camellias, and rhododendrons bloom in this 155-acre garden. Twelve miles of pathways wind through the Japanese, Wildflower Meadow, Renaissance, Colonial Herb, and Healing Gardens. Guided tram and boat tours are available.

Norfolk Naval Station, 9079 Hampton Boulevard, 757-444-7955.

Home port to more than 100 ships, this is the largest naval installation in the world. Guided bus tours pass by aircraft carriers and submarines. During the weekend, the base offers tours of selected ships. You can board the tour bus at the Naval Base Tour Office, 9809 Hampton Boulevard.

Yorktown

This small village on the bank of the York River witnessed the end of the American Revolution in 1781. In the Yorktown home of Augustine Moore, commissioners wrote the terms by which Cornwallis's British forces surrendered to George Washington's allied American and French forces and established American independence. You can walk along the river, through the preserved colonial town, and through Revolutionary and Civil War battlefields.

Appendix B: Contact Information

Throughout this book, we have advised you to contact local attractions, museums, and shops to confirm opening times, locations, and entrance fees. The list below gives you the phone numbers and addresses of the places we mentioned and other sites of interest. Hours and admission fees are subject to change.

Visitor information centers in Virginia Beach, Norfolk, Hampton, and Williamsburg house a wealth of information about the area. Staff will be happy to answer your questions if you visit or call.

Virginia Beach

Department of Parks and Recreation
Building 21
Virginia Beach, VA 23456
757-563-1100

Kempsville Area Library
832 Kempsville Road
Virginia Beach, VA 23464
757-495-1016

Virginia Beach Central Library
4100 Virginia Beach Boulevard
Virginia Beach, VA 23452
757-431-3000

Visitor Information Center
2100 Parks Avenue
Virginia Beach, VA 23451
800-446-8038
Event information: 757-499-SUNN
Hotel reservations: 800-VA-BEACH
www.virginia-beach-va.us, www.vbfun.com

Open 9 A.M. to 8 P.M. Memorial Day through Labor Day, 9 A.M. to 5 P.M. in the off-season. Closed Thanksgiving, Christmas, and New Year's Day.

Activities, Attractions, and Museums

Adam Thoroughgood House
1636 Parish Road
Virginia Beach, VA 23455
757-460-0007

Open Tuesday through Saturday 10 A.M. to 5 P.M., Sunday 1 P.M. to 5 P.M. Final tour begins at 4:30 P.M. Admission fee, free for children under 5.

Association for Research and Enlightenment
67th Street and Atlantic Avenue
P.O. Box 595
Virginia Beach, VA 23451–0595
757-428-3588

Open Monday through Saturday 9 A.M. to 8 P.M., Sunday 11 A.M. to 8 P.M. Tours, group ESP demonstrations, 30-minute movie, and free lecture offered daily.

Atlantic Wildfowl Heritage Museum
1113 Atlantic Avenue
Virginia Beach, VA 23451
757-437-8432

Open Tuesday through Saturday 10 A.M. to 5 P.M., Sunday noon to 5 P.M. Free admission.

Back Bay National Wildlife Refuge
4005 Sandpiper Road
Virginia Beach, VA 23456
757-721-2412
TDD: 1-800-828-1120
Tram: 757-498-BIRD

Open daily sunrise to sunset. Closed all federal holidays except Memorial Day, Independence Day, and Labor Day. Parking fee.

Cape Henry Lighthouse/Association for the Preservation of Virginia Antiquities
4401 Wishart Road
Virginia Beach, VA 23455–5524
757-422-9421
Open daily 10 A.M. to 5 P.M., March 15 to October 31. Admission fee.

Cavalier Hotels
42nd Street and Oceanfront
Virginia Beach, VA 23451
800-446-8199, 757-425-8555
Tours of Cavalier on the Hill by appointment only.

Church Point Manor House
4001 Church Point Road
Virginia Beach, VA 23455
757-460-2657

Contemporary Art Center of Virginia
2200 Parks Avenue
Virginia Beach, VA 23451
757-425-0000

Open weekdays 10 A.M. to 5 P.M., Saturday 10 A.M. to 4 P.M., Sunday noon to 4 P.M. Free admission.

False Cape State Park
4001 Sandpiper Road
Virginia Beach, VA 23456
757-426-7128

Open all day, every day, but unless you arrive by boat, you must pass through Back Bay National Wildlife Refuge. See Back Bay (above) for hours and parking fees.

Farmer's Market
3640 Dam Neck Road
Virginia Beach, VA 23456
757-427-4395
TDD: 757-427-4305

Open all day, every day; special events Friday and Saturday evenings during the summer.

First Landing/Seashore State Park and Natural Area
2500 Shore Drive
Virginia Beach, VA 23451
757-481-2131

Open daily from dawn to dusk. Visitor center open 10 A.M. to 6 P.M. Parking fee, except free on Wednesdays.

Fort Story U.S. Army Base
Post Headquarters, Building 300
Fort Story, VA 23459
757-422-7755

Open daily to the public 5 A.M. to 11 P.M.

Francis Land House
3131 Virginia Beach Boulevard
Virginia Beach, VA 23452
757-431-4000

Open Tuesday through Saturday 9 A.M. to 5 P.M., Sunday noon to 5 P.M. Admission fee.

Lynnhaven House
4401 Wishart Road
Virginia Beach, VA 23455
757-460-1688

Open Tuesday through Sunday, noon to 4 P.M., from June through September; weekends during May and October. Admission fee.

Oceana Naval Air Station
Oceana Boulevard
Virginia Beach, VA
757-433-3131

Observation parks open all day, every day. Call for base hours.

Old Coast Guard Station
24th Street and Atlantic Avenue
Virginia Beach, VA 23451
757-422-1587

Open Monday through Saturday 10 A.M. to 5 P.M., Sunday noon to 5 P.M. Closed Mondays after Labor Day and before Memorial Day. Admission fee.

Pavilion Convention Center
1000 19th Street
Virginia Beach, VA 23451
Event information: 757-428-8000, 757-437-4774

Hours and admissions vary by event.

Virginia Beach Amphitheater
3550 Cellar Door Way
Virginia Beach, VA 23456
Concert information: 757-368-3000
Tickets: 757-671-8100
www.cellardoor.com

Virginia Beach Fishing Pier
Oceanfront at 15th Street
Virginia Beach, VA 23451
757-428-2333

Open all day, every day. Admission fee.

Virginia Beach Municipal Center
North Landing Road
Virginia Beach, VA 23456
757-427-4111

Public information office, city hall, and other municipal buildings open weekdays 8:30 A.M. to 5 P.M.

Virginia Marine Science Museum
717 General Booth Boulevard
Virginia Beach, VA 23451
757-425-3474
TDD: 757-427-4305

Open daily 9 A.M. to 5 P.M. Call for extended summer hours. Closed Thanksgiving and Christmas. Admission fee. Separate movie admission. Combination tickets available.

City Parks

Elizabeth River Park
Challedon Drive
Virginia Beach, VA
Open daily sunrise to sunset. No park office.

Mount Trashmore
300 Edwin Drive
Virginia Beach, VA 23455
757-473-5237

Open daily 7:30 A.M. to 8:30 P.M., except Christmas.

Princess Anne Park
Princess Anne Road and Dam Neck Road
Virginia Beach, VA 23456
757-427-6020

Open daily 7 A.M. to sunset, except Christmas.

Red Wing Park
1398 General Booth Boulevard
Virginia Beach, VA 23451
757-437-4847

Open daily 7:30 A.M. to sunset, except Christmas.

Virginia Beach Parks Leisure Events
300 Edwin Drive
Virginia Beach, VA 23462

To reserve picnic shelters at all parks, call 757-473-5251 weekdays, 10 A.M. to 3 P.M.

Hotels
Virginia Beach Visitor Information Center
Reservations: 1-800-446-8038

Shopping
Lynnhaven Mall
701 Lynnhaven Parkway
Virginia Beach, VA 23454
757-340-9340

Pembroke Mall
4582 Pembroke
Virginia Beach, VA 23462
757-497-6255

Transportation
Beach Taxi
757-486-4304

Airport Shuttle
Groome Transportation
757-857-1231

Norfolk-Virginia Beach International Airport
757-857-3351 2200
Norview Avenue
Norfolk, VA 23518

Tidewater Regional Transit
1500 Monticello Avenue
Norfolk, VA 23510
757-640-6300
TDD: 757-640-6255
www.ridetrt.org

Buses operate seven days a week and are lift-equipped for people with disabilities. Call for schedule and fare information.

Norfolk

Norfolk Visitor Information Center
232 East Main Street
Norfolk, VA 23510
1-800-368-3097, 757-664-6620
Event information: 757-441-2345
www.norfolk.va.us, www.festeventsva.org

Open daily 9 A.M. to 6 P.M. Memorial Day through Labor Day, 9 A.M. to 5 P.M. in the off-season. Closed Christmas and Thanksgiving.

Activities, Attractions, and Museums

American Rover **Tour Ship**
757-627-SAIL

Tall sailing ship offering harbor tours, departs from Waterside Festival Marketplace. Call for schedule and prices.

Carrie B Tour Boat
757-393-4735

Paddlewheeler offering tours of the Elizabeth River, departs from Waterside Festival Marketplace at noon, 2 P.M., and 6 P.M. Cost depends on length of cruise.

Christ and St. Luke's Episcopal Church
560 Olney Road
Norfolk, VA 23507
757-627-5665

Open Monday through Friday 10 A.M. to 2 P.M., Saturday 10 A.M. to noon. Call for Sunday service schedule.

Chrysler Museum of Art
245 West Olney Road
Norfolk, VA 23510-1587
757-664-6200

www.whro.org/cl/cmhh

Open Tuesday through Saturday 10 A.M. to 5 P.M., Sunday 1 P.M. to 5 P.M. Closed New Year's Day, Independence Day, Thanksgiving, and Christmas Day. Admission fee, free to all on Wednesday.

Hunter House Victorian Museum
240 West Freemason Street
Norfolk, VA 23510
757-623-9814

Open April through December, Wednesday through Saturday 10 A.M. to 3:30 P.M., Sunday 12:30 P.M. to 3:30 P.M. Closed Monday, Tuesday, and major holidays. Admission fee.

MacArthur Memorial
Norfolk, VA 23510
757-441-2965

Open Monday through Saturday 10 A.M. to 5 P.M., Sunday
11 A.M. to 5 P.M. Closed New Year's Day, Thanksgiving and
Christmas Day. Free admission.

Moses Myers House
331 Bank Street
Norfolk, VA 23510
757-664-6200

Open Tuesday through Saturday 10 A.M. to 5 P.M., Sunday
1 P.M. to 5 P.M. Closed Mondays. Tours on the hour and
half-hour. Call for admission fee.

Nauticus, the National Maritime Center
Waterside Drive
Norfolk, VA 23510
757-664-1000
www.nauticus.org

Open daily Memorial Day through Labor Day, 10 A.M. to 5
P.M. During the off-season, open Tuesday through Saturday
10 A.M. to 5 P.M., Sunday noon to 5 P.M. Closed Thanksgiving, Christmas, and New Year's Day. Admission fee, free for
children 5 and under, discount for military personnel and
seniors.

Norfolk Botanical Garden
6700 Azalea Garden Road
Norfolk, VA 23518
757-441-5830

Open daily April 15 to October 15, 9 A.M. to 7 P.M. Open
daily October 16 to April 14, 9 A.M. to 5 P.M. Admission fee,
free for children under 5.

Norfolk Naval Station Tour Office
9079 Hampton Boulevard
Norfolk, VA 23505
757-444-7955

Tours daily except Thanksgiving, Christmas, and New Year's Day. Admission fee.

St. Paul's Episcopal Church
210 St. Paul's Boulevard
Norfolk, VA 23501
757-627-4353

Churchyard open all day, every day; church open for self-guided tours Tuesday through Friday, 9:30 A.M. to 4 P.M. Call church office to arrange guided tours and for service schedule.

***Spirit of Norfolk* Tour Boat**
Otter Berth at the Waterside
Norfolk, VA
757-627-7771

Lunch and dinner cruises Monday through Sunday. Midnight cruises Friday and Saturday.

Tugboat Museum
Waterside Festival Marketplace
Norfolk, VA 23510
757-627-4884

Open daily Memorial Day through Labor Day, 10 A.M. to 7 P.M. Open off-season Tuesday through Sunday, 11 A.M. to 6 P.M. Admission fee.

Waterside Festival Marketplace
333 Waterside Drive
Norfolk, VA 23510
757-627-3300

Open Monday through Saturday 10 A.M. to 9 P.M. (10 P.M. in summer), Sunday noon to 6 P.M. (8 P.M. in summer). Restaurants and entertainment facilities may stay open later.

Willoughby-Baylor House
601 East Freemason Street
Norfolk, VA 23510
757-664-6200

Open by appointment only.

Hampton

Hampton Visitor Center
710 Settlers Landing Road
Hampton, VA 23669
1-800-800-2202, 757-800-2202, 757-727-1102
www.hampton.va.us/tourism

Open daily 9 A.M. to 5 P.M. Closed Thanksgiving, Christmas, and New Year's Day.

Activities, Attractions, and Museums

Casemate Museum/Fort Monroe
P.O. Box 341
Fort Monroe, VA 23651
757-727-3391

Museum open daily 10:30 A.M. to 4:30 P.M. Closed Thanksgiving, Christmas, and New Year's Day.

Fort open all day, every day. Free admission.

Hampton Carousel
602 Settlers Landing Road
Hampton, VA 23369
757-727-6347

From March 28 to September 30, operates Monday through Saturday, 10 A.M. to 8 P.M., and Sunday noon to 6 P.M.; from October 1 to November 30, operates daily from noon to 6 P.M. Open weekends through December 15.

Hampton University
Ogden Circle
Hampton, VA 23668
757-727-5000

Offices open Monday through Friday, 8 A.M. to 5 P.M.

Hampton University Museum
Hampton University Campus
Ogden Circle
Hampton, VA 23668
757-727-5308

Open Monday through Friday 8 A.M. to 5 P.M., Saturday and Sunday noon to 4 P.M. Closed major holidays and campus holidays. Free admission.

***Miss Hampton II* Tour Boat**
710 Settlers Landing Road
Hampton, VA 23669
1-800-800-2202, 757-800-2202, 757-727-1102

Three-hour cruises depart from Hampton Visitor Center daily April through October at 10 A.M.; Memorial Day through Labor Day, 10 A.M. and 2 P.M. Admission fee, free for children 5 and younger.

St. John's Episcopal Church
100 West Queens Way
Hampton, VA 23669
757-722-2567

Open weekdays 9 A.M. to 3:30 P.M., Saturday 9 A.M. to noon. Sunday services are at 8, 9, 9:30, and 10:30 A.M. Summer services daily at 8 and 10 A.M. Free admission.

Virginia Air & Space Center
600 Settlers Landing Road
Hampton, VA 23669
1-800-296-0800, 757-727-0900
www.vasc.org

From Memorial Day to Labor Day, open Monday through Wednesday, 10 A.M. to 5 P.M., Thursday through Sunday, 10 A.M. to 7 P.M. From Labor Day to Memorial Day, open Mondays through Sundays, 10 A.M. to 5 P.M. Closed Thanksgiving and Christmas. Admission fee. Separate IMAX theater admission. Combination discounts available.

Williamsburg

Colonial Williamsburg Foundation
P.O. Box 1776
Williamsburg, VA 23187–8938
800-HISTORY, 757-220-7645
TTY: 757-565-8938
www.colonialwilliamsburg.org/travel

Open daily 9:30 A.M. to 5 P.M. Call for hours of various attractions. Cost of entrance pass depends on the number of days and the number of exhibition buildings and museums you wish to visit. Children under 6 are free.

Jamestown

Association for the Preservation of Virginia Antiquities
204 West Franklin Street
Richmond, VA 23220
804-648-1889

Colonial National Historical Park/Jamestown
Virginia Route 614 and the Colonial Parkway
P.O. Box 210
Yorktown, VA 23690
Visitor center: 757-898-3400
www.nps.gov/col

Open daily 8:30 A.M. until dusk. Visitor center open daily 9 A.M. to 5 P.M. except major holidays. Admission valid for a week.

Jamestown Settlement
Yorktown-Jamestown Foundation
P.O. Box JF
Williamsburg, VA 23187
757-253-7300

Open daily 9 A.M. to 5 P.M. except Christmas Day and New Year's Day. Admission fee.

Other Area Attractions

Yorktown Victory Center
Old State Route 238
P.O. Box 1607
Williamsburg, VA 23187–1607
757-887-1776

Open 9 A.M. to 5 P.M. daily, except Christmas Day and New Year's Day. Admission fee.

Appendix C: Great Tastes

Virginia Beach and the surrounding area offer hundreds of restaurants specializing in fresh seafood and diverse cuisine. Have fun and explore the many choices. The restaurants listed below are local favorites.

Virginia Beach

Coyote Cafe Cantina
972 Laskin Road
Virginia Beach, VA 23451
757-425-8705

Creative collection of Southwestern and other cuisine at reasonable prices. The corncake with salsa is a favorite.

Rudee's Restaurant and Raw Bar
227 Mediterranean Avenue
Virginia Beach, VA 23451
757-425-1777

For fresh local seafood, reasonably priced and prepared in traditional ways, Rudee's cannot be beat. Adjacent to a marina on Rudee Inlet.

Steinhilbers
653 Thalia Road
Virginia Beach, VA 23454
757-340-1156

This seafood restaurant has been around for years, hidden in one of Virginia Beach's older neighborhoods. If you enjoy fried shrimp, don't even bother to look at the menu—Steinhilbers offers some of the best you will ever eat.

Tautogs Restaurant
205 23rd Street
Virginia Beach, VA 23451
757-422-0081

Tautogs is housed in Winston's Cottage, a historic cottage in the resort area. Take a look at the bar, which was constructed from the doors of the upstairs rooms. The fireplace warms the cottage during cool months, and the front porch is a great place to dine during warm months. Seafood is the specialty.

Norfolk

Freemason Abbey
209 West Freemason Street
Norfolk, VA 23510
757-622-3966

A traditional American menu in a 124-year-old renovated church.

Thyme Square
509 Botetourt Street
Norfolk, VA 23501
757-623-5082

For a light and fresh lunch in a casual atmosphere.

Hampton

Magnolia House
232 South Armistead Avenue
Hampton, VA 23669
757-722-6881

Breakfast and lunch are served in this charming Victorian house. A walk around the antique shop upstairs will help you to digest.

Appendix D: Useful Phone Numbers

Central Library:
757-431-3000

Fire Department:
emergency 911, non-emergency 757-427-4228

Lynnhaven Parkway Post Office:
757-340-6227

Parks and Recreation Department:
757-563-1100

Police Department:
emergency 911, non-emergency 757-427-5616

Public Information Office:
757-427-4111, (TDD) 757-427-4305

Sentara Norfolk General Hospital:
757-668-3201

Tidewater Regional Transit:
757-640-6300, (TDD) 757-640-6255

Virginia Beach General Hospital:
757-481-8383

Virginia Highway Helpline:
800-367-ROAD

The Virginian-Pilot **(daily newspaper):**
757-446-2000

Virginia Relay Center:
800-828-1140, 800-828-1120 (TDD)

Visitor Information Center:
800-VA-BEACH, 757-437-4888 (for hotel reservations)

Weather:
757-666-1212

Western Union:
800-325-6000

Appendix E: Read All About It

If you want to learn more about the area, the following books will provide information on history, nature, culture, and social life. Enjoy!

Nonfiction

The Beach: A History of Virginia Beach, Virginia. Revised edition, 1996. Produced by the Virginia Beach Public Library, based on original text by Kathleen M. Eighmey.

  Information on everything from pirates to lighthouses to the military.

Lippson, Alice Jane, and Lippson, Robert L. *Life in the Chesapeake Bay.* Baltimore: The Johns Hopkins University Press, 1984.

  An illustrated guide to plants, fish, invertebrates, birds, and other animals of the local bays and inlets.

Mansfield, Stephen. *Princess Anne County and Virginia Beach: A Pictorial History.* Virginia Beach: The Donning Company, 1989.

  Hundreds of photographs of Virginia Beach and Princess Anne County.

Venable, Louisa Kyle. *A Country Woman's Scrapbook.* Virginia Beach: JCP Corporation of Virginia, 1980.

  An illustrated journal covering history, social life, and customs.

——. *The Witch of Pungo and Other Historical Stories of the Early Colonies.* Virginia Beach: Four O'clock Farms Publishing Co., 1973.

  Although this book is cataloged as juvenile fiction, it provides a simple portrait of life in colonial Virginia.

Fiction

Barth, John. *The Tidewater Tales: A Novel.* New York: Putnam, 1987.

　　During a sailing trip, a couple tells stories about the sea, sex, navigation, and narration; includes details of crabbing and fishing on Chesapeake Bay.

Cornwell, Patricia. *Cause of Death.* New York: G.P. Putnam's Sons, 1996.

　　Dr. Kay Scarpetta unravels what happened to a reporter who was murdered while investigating a story in the waters of the Elizabeth River.

Haley, Wendy. *Shadow Whispers.* New York: Kensington Publishing, 1992.

　　This thriller traces a psychopath's journey through the alleys of Norfolk.

Hoffman, William, *Tidewater Blood.* Chapel Hill, NC: Algonquin Books of Chapel Hill, 1998.

　　A mystery about the estranged son of a wealthy Virginia family who lives in a cabin on Chesapeake Bay.

Styron, William. *A Tidewater Morning: Three Tales from Youth.* New York: Random House, 1993.

　　Three stories about the author at the ages of ten, thirteen, and twenty set in coastal Virginia.

——. *Lie Down in Darkness.* Indianapolis: Bobbs-Merrill, 1951.

　　Set between World Wars I and II, this story depicts the disintegration of a family.

Appendix F: Walking Clubs

Gator Volksmarsch Club
P.O. Box 14025
Norfolk, VA 23518
757-523-1614

This club is part of the American Volkssport Association, a network of clubs that sponsor noncompetitive walking, swimming, in-line skating, and bicycling events. The local club sponsors four events each year. For information, contact the local Volksmarsch club or the American Volkssport Association at 800-830-WALK.

Tidewater Striders
1705 Colley Avenue
Norfolk, VA 23507
757-627-RACE

The Tidewater Striders promote running, walking, and multisport events for people of all ages and athletic abilities. They maintain a race schedule of approximately 60 events a year, including walking events. For an event schedule, call 757-627-RACE.

Index

208

Index

Meet the Author

Katherine Jackson has walked the Boardwalk, beaches, and trails of Virginia Beach since she moved to the area in 1976. She has also traveled extensively and walked in Belize, Costa Rica, Kenya, and Peru, as well as in more than half of the United States.

Jackson worked in public relations for 15 years before leaving her most recent position with the Virginia Beach Public Information Office to pursue a master's degree at Old Dominion University and several writing projects. She has written numerous articles for professional publications, and she recently wrote a piece on the Outer Banks of North Carolina for *The Surfer's Journal.*

PHOTO BY JULIE DUNLAP